Colin Hogg (born Dunedin, New Zealand, 1950, to Scottish immigrant parents) is a writer best known for his music journalism, reviewing and column writing, and for his biographical books and his television documentaries.

He has won a New Zealand Children's Book Award, a New Zealand Television Award for scriptwriting and a British High Commission Travel Writing Award.

Hogg grew up in Dunedin and Invercargill where he joined *The Southland Times* as a cadet reporter at the age of 17. By the end of the 1960s, he was writing about music for the paper before departing for Auckland, *The New Zealand Herald* and *The Auckland Star*, where he established himself as an opinionated byline writer.

He wrote a humorous column about being a man for the *New Zealand Woman's Weekly* off and on for 30 years and also worked in television as a writer, producer and occasional presenter and director.

By the same author

*Living with Summer* (1983)

*Angel Gear: On the road with Sam Hunt* (1989)

*Is That an Affair on Your Mind or
Are You Just Glad to See Me?* (1997)

*Cinema: A world history* (1998)

*The Awful Truth: An unauthorised autobiography* (1998)

*The Zoo: Meet the locals* (2000)

*A Life in Loose Strides: The story of Barry Crump* (2000)

# GOING SOUTH

## A ROAD TRIP THROUGH LIFE

COLIN HOGG

HarperCollins*Publishers*

**HarperCollins*Publishers***

First published in 2015
by HarperCollins*Publishers* (New Zealand) Limited
Unit D1, 63 Apollo Drive, Rosedale, Auckland 0632, New Zealand
harpercollins.co.nz

**HarperCollins*Publishers***
Unit D1, 63 Apollo Drive, Rosedale, Auckland 0632, New Zealand
Level 13, 201 Elizabeth Street, Sydney NSW 2000
A 53, Sector 57, Noida, UP, India
1 London Bridge Street, London, SE1 9GF, United Kingdom
2 Bloor Street East, 20th floor, Toronto, Ontario M4W 1A8, Canada
195 Broadway, New York NY 10007, USA

A catalogue record for this book is available from the National Library of New Zealand.

ISBN 978 1 7755 4081 6 (pbk)
ISBN 978 1 7754 9118 7 (ebook)

'Hitting Forty' by Sam Hunt reproduced with the permission of the poet

Front cover photograph by Gordon McBride; all other photography by
Gordon McBride and Colin Hogg
Cover design by areadesign.co.nz
Typeset in Sabon LT by Kirby Jones
Printed and bound in Australia by Griffin Press
The papers used by HarperCollins in the manufacture of this book are a natural, recy-
clable product made from wood grown in sustainable plantation forests. The fibre source
and manufacturing processes meet recognised international environmental standards, and
carry certification.

*the world is held together*
*by cobwebs*
**Sam Hunt**

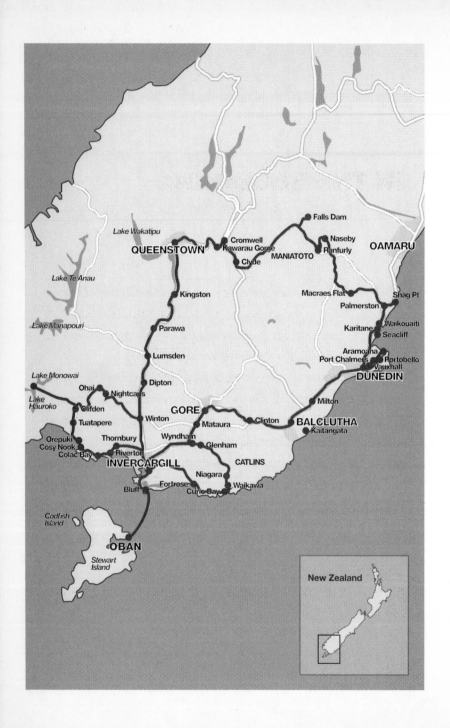

# IN THE BEGINNING

It was late afternoon and a few of us were sitting about in the sun having a drink on my birthday when the friend I've known the longest sat down opposite and looked at me like he was going to say something serious.

He was, and he got straight to it. He had health issues, he said, in a tone that put the 'issues' word in ironic quotes. He's an ironic guy, only a couple of months younger than me. We started work on the same small-city New Zealand newspaper 46 years ago, which seems quite ridiculous to both of us now. I'd told him earlier how less than happy I was about my new age and how angry at that damn Beatles song. But now the talk was serious.

He'd been to see his doctor the previous day, he said, and, not to piss around the post, he had cancer and it was terminal, and there was nothing that could really be done about it except some chemo at some point to slow it down. He had maybe a year, he said. Maybe a bit more.

The others at my little birthday party couldn't hear what was going on between us, and Gordon was intent on telling me his dreadful news like it was something he wanted to get out so he didn't have to talk to me about it ever again.

I was so shocked by what he told me that, after an initial gasp, I said the only thing that seemed to make any sense to me in the circumstances. 'We should go away for a road trip,' I blurted out.

He nodded as if he knew I was going to say that. 'Back south,' he said.

'Yeah,' I said back to him.

'South' meant Southland, where our story started, as mentioned, 46 years earlier. And that was the end of that conversation. Within weeks the trip was all booked and ready to roll. I felt nervous.

My ironic friend's name is Gordon McBride. Like me, he's what we used to call a scribbler, and it's still the description I like best. I first encountered him, fresh-faced in the Reporters' Room of *The Southland Times* around the middle of 1968, a great year to turn 18, which we both did then. I'd started at the paper as a cadet reporter in February that year, a nervous fool in my new Italian-cut suit, bought specially, with a bit of help from Mum, from Hallensteins Menswear, down the road.

I got the job, I think, because I touched a happy place in the newspaper's editor's heart. The editor had a terrific name: Jack Grimaldi. In the midst of the interview, he'd asked what sports interested me, and I'd said golf because that's what I'd played at my Invercargill high school. I'd taken up golf only because of my failings at what are often whimsically referred to as 'contact sports'. It was odd that my school even offered golf, but it did, and just as well it did.

Because it turned out that Jack Grimaldi liked golf a great deal, and in fact he went on to die on his favourite golf course a few years after interviewing me. But in his smoky office that day, on the first floor of the *Southland Times* building with a view out over Invercargill's busy Esk Street, I saw his eyes light up when I said 'golf' and I had the feeling I was in.

Gordon must have said something else that impressed Jack Grimaldi, who was an editor of the old school — stocky and leathery and ancient-seeming, not unlike the old movie actor Edward G Robinson. I now recall only two things Mr Grimaldi ever said to me, apart from that question about golf.

On keeping things simple, he once instructed me, after I must have foolishly inserted a fancy word into some story I'd written, 'Fires aren't "extinguished", young Colin, they're "put out".' And then another time, a little later on, when the two of us were travelling together in the claustrophobic, slow and creaking metal lift up to the editorial department on the first floor, he leaned in towards me, smelling faintly of whisky, perhaps from lunch at his club, and rumbled, 'I hope you're getting enough greens to eat in that flat of yours, young Colin.'

And of course I wasn't getting anything like enough greens to eat in that flat of mine, which I'd recently moved into with the newest reporter in the office, young Thomas Gordon McBride, a bouncy farmer's son from Wyndham with a Beatles hair-do, a souped-up Mini and a lot more confidence than I had. But, like he did, I pretty much instantly fell in love with newspapers and the whole wayward world of scribblers.

We were both only kids, and if it seems odd enough that we should have been working as newspaper reporters aged only 17, it now seems even odder that we were each doing it while living away from the safety and comforts of our family nests.

Gordon had had to move out of his familiar boyhood bedroom at the old family farm, way out across the Southland Plains at a place called Glenham, near Wyndham, so he could take up his exciting new job in Invercargill. And my family, by wonderful coincidence, had moved away from Invercargill when my father landed a promotion to Christchurch soon after I'd started my job at the *Times*.

There was a failed attempt by my parents to take me to Christchurch, too. There was even a job lined up for me at a newspaper there, but I really didn't want to go and, after a fair bit of anguish from Mum, I'd been allowed to keep my job at *The Southland Times* and sent to board with an old couple who had a room to rent in their big old villa in a quiet part of Invercargill.

The old couple might have appreciated the $12 a week I paid them out of my $20 weekly wage, but they never adjusted to my working hours, which ran as late as two in the morning, and I didn't always go straight home afterwards. Going home to bed wasn't what a boy wanted to do immediately after all the excitement of making a newspaper. I was out of sync with everything.

It was the Invercargill tradition, in those days anyway, to serve dinner at midday rather than in the evening, so I'd rise to be greeted with soup, tripe and onions, and a hefty pudding. In the face of the tripe especially, so early in my day, I'd had to run swiftly for the bathroom a couple of times.

Gordon, it turned out, was suffering similar misunderstandings where he'd been put to board, so the two of us plotted together and somehow managed to reassure our worried mothers that we could look after ourselves. Then we tricked some foolish landlord into thinking we were responsible tenants and found ourselves a flat.

It was in the northern part of Invercargill, in the back bit of an old villa in a street called Dublin, behind some young cops who had the bigger flat in the front of the house. Our place was tiny, but we didn't care. We were kings of our domain, though we had to share the only bedroom. The bathroom was the biggest room in the place. The sitting

room was too tiny to actually sit down in. We had very little furniture anyway and often very little to eat.

We had a party the first Saturday to celebrate our new extended freedom. We invited some of the nurses who boarded at the nursing home at Invercargill's Kew Hospital. I don't know how we made the connection with them, but they were night workers like us, and also, as it turned out, quite a lot of fun. We had a pyjama party, though that might not have been the first night. There are old photos Gordon has. I have a moustache like a spotty Mexican bandit, and Gordon is caught in the picture yelling with glee while wearing what looks like an old lady's nightie.

One night we were invited over to a party at the cops' place next door, and repaid their neighbourly generosity by stealing their extensive and colourful collection of liqueur-filled miniatures and taking them back to our place and drinking the lot. I'm not sure if there were any nurses involved. We might have been nervous of nurses by then. I recall one of them telling me they had a pet axolotl that they kept in a tank at the nursing home and that they fed it the foreskins cut off the boy babies born at the hospital.

We upgraded after a while to a better, bigger flat, at the front of a high-set house right in the middle of town in classy Ythan Street, straight across the road from Invercargill's rather lovely brick Byzantine-styled First Church. This would turn out to be an unfortunate arrangement on several occasions.

There was a tiny sunroom at the front of the house, but Gordon's country cousin Fred used to crash there when he was in town, so the two of us shared a bedroom again.

We had parties most Saturdays, some of them quite wild, sometimes still involving nightwear. We often ran out of money and food, though we rarely ran out of beer or reasons to have parties — being Saturday always seemed reason enough.

At *The Southland Times*, Gordon pursued his natural reporting instincts and kept chasing the news of the day, while I joined the sub-editing team, where there was no dress code and I didn't have to interview uninteresting people. Also, rewriting other people's stories seemed the best way to learn to write. At 18, I was the newspaper's foreign editor, choosing, headlining and laying out the world news for the readers of Southland.

It was the time of the Irish Troubles, Vietnam, Charles Manson, and The Beatles getting weird. I didn't entirely know what I was doing, but I was sure learning fast. I was told off quite severely by Mr Grimaldi on one occasion for omitting the British Budget from the paper because I'd thought it too boring for words. Gordon still likes to quote what he regards as my greatest headline, 'Man On Moon', though I suspect he's being ironic.

Back at the flat, the parties continued at a merry pace. There were altercations with the local motorbike gang, and occasionally awful accusations from churchgoers when the festivities expanded too late into Sunday mornings.

That gang, the Antarctic Angels, were Invercargill's answer to America's Hells Angels. They crashed one of our parties. The big Angel banging on the door when I opened it had a dotted line tattooed across his throat with the words *Cut here*. He squished me into the hall wall with the front door before I could say anything about dress code or even introduce myself.

Gordie called for reinforcements from the flat next door, shouting through a handy little hatch door that interconnected the two halves of the house. There were several off-duty cops at our party anyway, and, after a while, the bikers were driven back out onto the street in front of the church while I got my breath back behind the door in the front hall. When I wandered out into the street, someone on our side handed me a broken bottle as the Antarctic Angels advanced on us. Gordie and I both emerged unscathed, though I don't know how.

It was a fun-filled and foolish time, and it's a wonder we survived some of the things that happened. We didn't call Gordon by his proper name back then. To us at the time he was Spud McBride, a sly reference to his Irish roots, I suppose.

But, even with that rustic nickname, he shone with a lot of natural, unstoppable charm. He liked the girls and the girls liked him, and after a while Spud had a fulltime girlfriend, Sheryl, who was lovely and always sweet to me, tirelessly trying to fix me up with dates, which never seemed to work out. She and Spud were really quite keen on each other. 'Is he asleep?' I'd hear her whisper, snuggled up with Spud in his single bed in the dark across the room. 'No, he bloody isn't,' I'd reply. Quickly. You had to be quick.

I wasn't immediately so lucky in love. I had a semi sort of girlfriend called Jane, who reckoned she was the abandoned daughter of some rich and famous family. She may have been a little deluded, but she didn't delude Spud.

He didn't like her much. 'She's a boat girl from Bluff,' he told me, but I didn't see it that way.

She was from Bluff, but she was cute all the same, a bit like Twiggy, I may have thought. She had one of those elfin haircuts that were all the go at the time, though not so much in Invercargill or, especially, Bluff. I tried to move her into the flat, but I came home from a night shift to find that Spud and his cousin had biffed her out. We moved into the garage together for a while, but it was too cold and damp.

Then a hot national pop band of the time, The Fourmyula, came to Invercargill for a concert and she went off with them for a few days, unsettling me a bit, and we drifted apart after that, though I missed the imported English cigarettes she used to get from the sailors on the freighters down at Bluff. They were Benson and Hedges. The English cigs tasted better. The reason was the tobacco was toasted. It said so on the packet.

Eventually I did get a proper girlfriend, but things were about to change anyway, closing the first chapter of my friendship with my friend from Wyndham. One day, without any warning that I can recall, Spud packed up and left the flat and our carefree life behind. Off he went to quietly marry Sheryl, move into their own house and raise the daughter they were about to have, and be a family and all that grown-up stuff.

We were 19. It was all a bit shocking and not the same anymore. Oh, and it was 1970.

Soon after Gordie moved out, I was suddenly moved out of the flat, too, evicted when the landlady, who by bad luck was also the local social welfare officer and never liked me anyway, caught me in the act of throwing out her lovely lounge suite, which had collapsed under the attentions of a particularly lively party the previous Saturday.

Also, I think some of her young female clients at Social Welfare might have mentioned our address in relation to parties they may have attended. So I moved on and found a new flat and new flatmates. We still had parties on Saturday nights. I even had my own room, but it wasn't quite as much fun without my old mate.

Within two years, I'd left Invercargill forever. Gordon left *The Southland Times* and went back, then left again, and we went off in different directions, vaguely keeping in touch as the decades drifted by and we cut our own grooves into something that we'd eventually come to think of, I suppose, as careers, careers being simply something you do over and over again for money.

Newspaper journalists, the ones who write that is, tend to gravitate in one of two directions — the driven fire-engine-chasing newshound type, or the lazier feature-writer type with opinions and a byline.

Gordie took the first path, while I took the second. He stayed true to the news and never turned to the dark pastures of public relations or political spin doctoring, as many of us did. He moved up through the ranks into leadership roles, something I never much aspired to, though I had a go a few times.

He was a fearless chief reporter at *The Christchurch Star* and, after moving to Wellington, chief reporter of *The Sunday Times* and associate chief reporter at *The*

*Dominion*, and he worked at *The National Business Review*. He was even briefly editor at one of the papers I worked on for eight years, *The Auckland Star*, as that poor old paper fell into its final death spiral in the 1980s.

Then Gordon took himself away from the newspapers and off into television and TV3, as first a news reporter and then a political reporter. I used to see him on the screen occasionally, and he was a natural and funny, too. He was interviewing Robert Muldoon for TV3 around the time I was interviewing ZZ Top for *The New Zealand Herald*.

Then Gordie moved up the ranks again and spent his last couple of working decades as the head of TV3's hell-for-leather news operation in Wellington. He was their rock in a hard place. His workmates called him Flash by then, as in Flash Gordon. He liked loud shirts. That young first marriage with Sheryl had lasted 12 years or so, and Gordie was in a happy new relationship with a great woman called Patricia. She was smarter than him, which was a good thing, but he was still smart. And he was still a handful when he'd had a few.

I'd stayed roughly true to the old trade, too, but I'd gone in that other direction. I was never much good at writing about news anyway. I wanted to get breathless about other things. From early on I was determined to indulge my secret desire to be a rock music writer. I'd grown up crazy about music, reading music mags and seeing the first generation of new music writers rising in England and America, and I didn't see why one couldn't rise in Invercargill, too.

I came from a family of immigrants, persistent people, and I figured if you persisted long enough with something, eventually someone will either surrender or indulge you, and eventually one of those is just what happened at *The Southland Times*.

What helped was a pre-existing page devoted to entertainment and music news and reviews each week in the newspaper's popular Saturday evening tabloid sports edition. I set my sights on it and, after a certain amount of mad pestering persistence and an odd unwavering self-belief, there I was, aged about 18, filling a page each week with stories about the glories of rock and roll, local, national and international. They even paid me for doing it, a whole extra four bucks a week. That would have covered the petrol for the Vespa. More than.

I reviewed records as if I knew what was what. I felt the best way to get attention was to have strong opinions. I arrived just in time to pass judgement on the last Beatles album, *Let It Be* — disappointing — and hail several Invercargill bands as the next great thing, though I don't think any of them even got to make a record.

Some of them had wonderful names, though. One was called Judas Embrace, another A Gentle Feeling and then there was the Unknown Blues, who played nothing but songs by London's The Pretty Things, a raucous hairy R&B band who had actually visited Invercargill and played a memorable show which I'd attended at the Civic Theatre and been deeply impressed by when I was still at high school.

The Pretty Things were on an English package show with Sandie Shaw, who sang in bare feet, and Eden Kane, who'd had a hit with a ballad called 'Boys Cry' and wore a white suit. Neither the song nor the suit endeared him to the Invercargill crowd. He looked like a poofter, some locals reckoned.

Perhaps catching the mood of the audience, Viv Prince, The Pretty Things' wild-eyed and drunken drummer, slipped out onto the back of the stage as poor Eden sang his white-suited heart out and, to our great excitement, started a fire that brought an old man in a uniform running on with an enormous fire extinguisher trying to stop the show and put the fire out. It was punk before punk.

But generally not many major bands ever made it all the way down to us in Invercargill, at the far edge of the civilised world. When they did, they made an impact. I also saw the La De Das, fearsome at a sweaty Centennial Hall. Most importantly and best of all, I'd seen the young Rolling Stones play the Civic Theatre when I was 14, and heard them call us a bunch of 'sheep shearers' when the crowd kept shouting for Roy Orbison, who'd been on before them, to come back and do 'Only the Lonely' again.

Young Thomas Gordon McBride was at that concert, too, though I didn't know him then. Like me, he was there for the Stones rather than the Big O, as they called Roy in those days. Years later, when he got a little famous again in the 1980s, I managed to land an interview with Roy Orbison.

The first reason Roy became famous again was because 'In Dreams', perhaps the most breathtaking of all his breathtaking songs, was featured in a vivid and disturbing scene in the vivid and disturbing David Lynch movie *Blue Velvet*.

Roy told me he'd seen the movie and he really didn't know what to make of it, though he was very pleased to have his song used. A little while after that he became even more famous as a member of the Traveling Wilburys, the hugely successful folksy group he formed with his pals George Harrison, Bob Dylan, Tom Petty and Jeff Lynne. Talking to him, he seemed a very sweet man with impeccable manners. Though, as it was a telephone interview, for all I knew he might have been naked in a hot tub with The Staple Singers.

A few hundred interviews earlier, once I had my hands on that music page in Invercargill, I enthusiastically attempted to talk to any New Zealand bands who made it to town, poor devils. They may have been surprised by such attention, not to mention some of my nervous question lines. I took the local rock bands pretty seriously, too. In May of 1969, I wrote admonishingly in my newspaper:

> There was a disappointing attendance last Friday when A Gentle Feeling played at the first showing in Invercargill of The Beatles' full-length cartoon *Yellow Submarine*.
>
> Although the group was not up to its usual standard on a few of their songs, they put up a pretty solid performance and managed to fill the theatre with sound. A Gentle Feeling are improving all the time and their original and polished performances make them one of the outstanding local groups.

My favourite bit on the new job was reviewing records, and I'd proffer an opinion on anything I could get my hands on. The record companies, based up in Auckland and Wellington, mainly sent me the leftover review copies, the ones no one else wanted, the ones no one had really heard of.

But I didn't know this at the time and I was open to anything, so long as it was vinyl and it went round and round and made a noise. Therefore I took the new Lothar and the Hand People album as seriously as I took the West Coast Pop Art Experimental Band or the debut solo album by someone new called Neil Young. Our parties may well have had the most interesting, not to mention the newest, music in Invercargill at the time.

Shortly after turning 21, I packed all my records in my car and moved with my girlfriend and soon-to-be-wife to a job at *The New Zealand Herald* in far-off Auckland, and two years after that I went to London, where I stayed three years. Then I came back to Auckland and the *Herald* again, then *The Auckland Star*, where I got back into the music writing and managed to turn it into a fulltime job.

It was after I'd established myself as a record and show reviewer and rock star interviewer up in Auckland at the turn of the 1980s that Gordie took to occasionally ringing me up out of the blue in the early hours. He'd usually be half-cut in a bar in Wellington, arguing with someone about who played what on which song when and wanting me to settle the matter with my apparently unassailable knowledge of such things.

Gordon had made a smart move, I thought, getting across to television. There wasn't all that much life left in newspapers by then, though that had been coming for a while. The truth is that the newspaper business was already on the start of the slide even way back when Gordie and I signed on in the late 1960s.

Soon after I joined *The Southland Times*, it took over the ailing evening paper, *The Southland Daily News*. For a few years they printed an evening edition to fill the gap, but that disappeared, too. Up the line in Dunedin, *The Evening News* had already died and, later in Christchurch, the feisty *Christchurch Star* went down eventually. In Auckland, when I joined *The Auckland Star* in the late 1970s, it was already faltering, being slowly killed by television and other modern evening entertainments. Mostly by television, though.

There was a distinct upside to the downside, however. Working on a paper that was increasingly worried about its survival meant that the people in charge were open to almost any ideas that might attract readers, especially young ones.

At *The Auckland Star* they launched a daily entertainment section, and I started writing music stuff for it and running it, too, after a while. Then they launched a full-blown daily feature section which I was put in charge of. At one mad point, I had a staff of 16, including several ancient and cynical veterans.

We had an unprecedented amount of fun while somehow managing to keep our work standards up, though I couldn't help noticing increasing evidence that it came at a cost. A lot of us drank too much, and sometimes drank so much that we'd fall out or even sleep with each other when we shouldn't have. But consequences didn't count so much then, and, besides, we thought the good times would never end.

But they did end. It was when, somewhere behind a closed door one day, the accountants finally won the holy, never-ending war with the editorial department and set about killing the once bold and beloved *Auckland Star*, not all of a sudden, but by a thousand cuts. Editors came and went. I went, too, several times. Before it was all over, I'd worked for the *Star* three different times, and the *Herald* three times, too.

In the late 1980s, as mentioned, things had turned so strange that Gordon was moved up from Wellington by the company that now owned the paper and was briefly appointed the *Auckland Star* editor, which put us back in touch with each other again. But I'd gone back to the *Herald* by then and refused to take his job offers seriously. It just didn't seem right that the guy who used to sleep in the bed across the room from me should be my editor.

It was after that when he gave up on newspapers, went into television and moved back to Wellington. I stayed in Auckland and, not liking newspaper offices much anymore, went freelance. Eventually, I drifted into TV, too, when I figured out that making documentaries was a bit like writing feature stories. They just involved more electricity and people pointing cameras, and it took longer to make them. But the money was good, and there was still some of that precious stuff, freedom.

Sometime in the 1990s, Gordie was up in Auckland for a day and we made contact and met for lunch at one of those upmarket restaurants down on the city's waterfront. It must have been summer because I remember it was sunny. We ate Bluff oysters and drank a lot of wine.

I know that last bit because I had an alcohol-assisted rush of blood to the head and came up with the idea that we should go for a bit of a road trip together sometime, back down south. But, I emphasised to him, we needed a reason to go. Trips are always better when there's a reason. Then I promptly forgot about the conversation.

But Gordie didn't forget. He's not only a rock, he's an elephant. Independently, he decided we should go to Central Otago, and he announced this when a few weeks later he rang me out of the blue at two in the morning and woke me up.

We were, according to him, going to Naseby, where we could do some curling if we went in the winter. He'd booked a pub for us to stay at and everything. But I wasn't so sure curling was a good enough idea, and I didn't go in the end. But he went anyway, taking some of his new Wellington mates, and turning it into an annual event involving curling and running up massive bar tabs.

He kept on inviting me for a few years, but after a bit he gave up and stopped asking. I had cold feet about the curling, though I didn't tell him that. Also I felt we might get into some sort of trouble. I had kids by then, and perhaps I was trying to put bad behaviour behind me at the time. I probably remembered some of the madness we got up to when we were running together back in Invercargill, and worried that it might spontaneously combust again and there might be injuries or arrests.

But still the two of us would make some sort of contact every year or so, though we'd only rarely see each other. And the time rolled by, faster and faster, as it does, just like the old folk warned us it would, though we didn't believe them.

Over the years, I have been married, officially or otherwise, three times, and become father to five girls and a boy, and now, incredibly, grandfather (though we don't use that word) to four, shortly five, grandchildren. All my kids are grown up now and off in several parts of the world with their own lives.

Well, all except the youngest, who's 16, still at school and living at home with me and her mother, who I've been with for 22 years, bless her. We decided we liked each other so much that we even got married a few years ago. Things seemed settled, life went on, running straight ahead, it seemed, into the rest of the future.

Then, just when I was expecting nothing to happen, everything changed, as it does sometimes. Right out of the blue, we moved to Wellington, which was about the last thing I expected after living 40-odd years in Auckland, having up to that point enjoyed quite a nice fat career doing pretty much what I liked most and being paid quite a lot for doing it.

But I really should have seen it coming. Nothing was quite the same anymore, especially in the scribbling business I'd been in for so long. Now it wasn't so free and easy. Now I was older, I'd been doing what I'd been doing for rather a long time and my relevance, work-wise at least, was less relevant in an endlessly relevant business.

The last bit of the good times had been quite good, though. On the back of getting a couple of series commissioned by TVNZ, I'd started my own TV production company, taken a lease on an office on fashionable Ponsonby Road, employed regular staff, made good money, had lots of business lunches, bought a Mercedes-Benz, and started wondering what my next trick might be. Up to that point, there always had been a new trick.

But then it turned out that there was no new trick. After a few years of making them, my sorts of TV shows — documentaries and series about books and such — weren't the sorts of TV shows the big TV channels wanted anymore. I was being a bit too arty when everything was turning to reality and cooking and singing contests, the stuff of children. I could see the end coming, so I walked towards it, made my last show, shut my company down, had a last big wrap party, said goodbye to the staff and went home.

At first, I was more relieved than mournful. I thought I'd go back to writing for print, where I'd started out. But I should have looked more closely. The old business was really dying now, moving from critical to terminal, the country's newspapers and magazines fading faster and faster, as they were around the modern world. I'd turned back only to find myself chasing an outgoing tide. Everything was downsizing, including me.

After never missing a deadline across 30 years, my column and I were dropped by *Woman's Weekly*. The editor, another new one, rang and said I didn't fit anymore because the magazine was chasing a new demographic, something faintly disturbing called the 'yummy mummy'. I didn't know what to say to that.

The editor said she knew I'd understand and I said I did, but I didn't really, and perhaps neither did she because, within a few months, she was gone, too. Inside a year, I wasn't being recognised anymore by older ladies in supermarkets, which was a shame. I quite liked being recognised by them. They used to be my key demographic, I suspect.

'I know who you are,' they'd say to me up the cereal aisle.

'So do I,' I'd say right back.

I loved my elderly lady readers and I miss them sometimes, usually in the supermarket.

After giving up on TV and losing the *WW* column, things went from slightly bad to worse at some pace, until my career had handily shrunk to the point where what was left could be put in my back pocket and taken almost anywhere, even to another city, which is just what happened. The only good thing, it seemed, that could be immediately said about the whole deal was that I'd be in the same town as my old pal Gordon.

It was my wife Philippa's new job that moved us to Wellington, and things didn't at first go very well. In fact they went bad fast, a bit like the winds in that part of the country. But at least Gordie and I caught up with each other. We had lunches and dinners and drinks. We went to each other's houses. We seemed to enjoy each other's company in a new, dare I say mature, way, though sometimes we were still so excited at being in each other's company that we drank too much.

Meanwhile, I tried to write my way through the changes in my life, thinking I might have a little fun with the heaviness, turn it into a column.

For decades, I'd been writing about myself and my kids for the magazine that had now dropped me so unkindly, and the habit was quite hard to shake.

But no one seemed to want to print that sort of thing anymore. Or their budgets didn't stretch to such fripperies. Or maybe the Auckland paper I offered it to didn't want the pieces I wrote because they were about an Aucklander moving to Wellington, which was unthinkable. And the Wellington paper I offered the columns to didn't want them because they were a bit rude about Wellington, which was unacceptable. It was a hopeless situation. Still, I'd always found that writing had saved me in some way, even if it never got out to readers.

## A LOST COLUMN

I didn't see it coming. I really didn't, and I like to think of myself as a prescient type. But still, I did not see it coming. And if I had, I might have run away.

After all, anything, I'd have figured, was preferable to moving to Wellington — a city I'd previously sworn I'd settle down in only post-mortem and, even then, reluctantly.

But, right out of the blue, my wife landed a job in Wellington. Me, being only semi-employed and able to do the little paid work I had from almost anywhere — including a parked car — there was little I could say and even less I could do.

My love and financial dependency made me silent, though the teenage daughter felt no such constraints when she heard we were about to abandon the steamy pleasures of Auckland for ... well, Wellington.

'I'm not living in that puddle,' she wailed at the news.

'Oh, do belt up,' I told her. 'It won't be so bad. I know people who seem to like it there.' Despite the wind and the hills, the earthquakes and the constant threat of tsunami.

But we were going and that was that, and selling a house in Auckland was no trouble at all — the last thing to stop us, in fact. And it didn't, selling within weeks to some lucky bastards and sending us — working wife, daughter, cat and dog — south, in dribs and drabs.

I was the last drab to leave the city I'd lived in and — yes, let's get it out — loved, off and on, for 40 years or so. If I'd ever considered moving south, I'd thought it would have been all the way, to the far south where I was born and grew until I escaped — straight to Auckland, the golden city.

And now I was trading gold for capital — Wellington and no way back.

I arrived prepared for hills. I was born in Dunedin, after all. I'd been to San Francisco. Until recently, I'd lived on the side of a volcano called Mt Albert.

Yes, I knew about hills. But in Wellington there live the sort of hills that other hills might admire. They don't undulate so much as tumble, and the roads that claw and wiggle their ways up, over, around and down these hills are often little more than glorified goat tracks, terrifying to arrivistes in oversized cars.

I was also prepared for wind and weather of a sideways variety, which was duly provided on my second day in town, even though, according to the calendar fluttering on the wall, it was the height of summer.

I'd driven straight through to Wellington from Auckland once the movers had taken our stuff — mountains of it — away to storage and the cleaners had moved in. Eight hours later, I found myself driving up a roller-coaster road to a suburb whimsically called Brooklyn, where wife and daughter had settled into our temporary accommodation, an old place on a hill, I'd been told. Something of an understatement, it turned out — the old place having the outlook of an eagle's nest and the ambience of a Hitchcock movie.

The path from road and letterbox up to front door might test a mountaineer. Not only that, it made its ridiculous way past neighbours' windows and doors, sometimes so closely I had to take care not to look in. I'd been in its bosom only a couple of days when Wellington gave me its first big shake. I was at my desk in the so-called sunroom, staring out the window at the time, but didn't feel remotely alarmed while the place shuddered and flexed its old wooden bones. The house had been hanging on up there, way above Brooklyn, for 100 years or so and wasn't about to fall down just yet. Well, that was my theory, and it did help a soft ex-Aucklander from panicking.

And at least living up on a cliff meant we were well out of reach of my big nature-based dread in our new hometown — a sudden tsunami. While the rest of town was being swept halfway to Masterton, we'd be high and dry.

I had to find comfort where I could as we adjusted to life in Wellington, camping in a temporary home as we tried to make sense of the eccentric local real estate market where there hardly seemed to be anything for sale. And if it was for sale, it needed to be approached with caution. Sections in the sought-after suburbs clustered around central Wellington often turned out to be not much bigger than the houses clinging to them.

And even when there seemed to be more land involved, you might be buying a backyard only a family of abseilers could love. And when you did think you'd spotted the perfect place, there was nowhere to put the cars or it lost the afternoon sun at two o'clock or there were airliners flying past your window. Or there was an 'extra high' rating on the chances of an earthquake-induced landslide. And then there's the wind which, as a neighbour smilingly told me, 'really only comes from two directions — north and south'.

I never liked to look too closely, but I grew to suspect that the people of Wellington are made differently from the louche and weak-legged citizens of Auckland. For a start, they must possess thighs like strainer posts.

While we were temporarily living up in that haunted house on that cliff in Brooklyn, there was a bar I liked to take a beer at, down the bottom of our road. Though simply saying that we lived on a road with a bar at the bottom of it fails to quite capture the truth of the geography. The road wasn't really a road at all, but rather an unmoving escalator without the steps.

If I were to stumble going down, I would have entered that bar much more swiftly than intended — and in need of something stronger than mere beer.

Getting back up, full of boutique ale, was an even more life-threatening challenge. By the time I made it to my letterbox, my heart was generally hammering like a runaway loco.

And of course I was only halfway there, the house being at the far end of that steep and winding goat track. By the time I got to the front door, a red and rasping ruin, I'd give the family the impression I'd had 10 too many to drink down there when what had really done me in was the climbing.

Tip-toeing down one evening, I looked across the road to see a woman going up, angled forward, parallel with the footpath, pushing a fully occupied two-seater pram. She appeared completely unperturbed by her exertions, as if pushing all those kilos of offspring and pram up a 30-degree angle was the most natural thing in the world to be doing — which it is, of course, in this part of the world.

That old house rattled all night like a casino. It was the wind, which, if it wasn't blowing this way, was blowing that way, even upwards and downwards at times.

The locals said it could be nice in Wellington after a southerly, which seemed a bit like the man on the rack suggesting he felt good when his torturer took a tea break. But the locals also made no apology for the weather. In fact, they tended to bring it up before a recent arrival could get a mention of it in. Not that I had much to say about Wellington weather except, perhaps, Good bloody grief.

Trying to write columns about the things going on around me was a habit I maybe had to get out of. I'd been doing it for a large part of my working life. If I added up all of those words about life with me and the kids for that one magazine, there might be a million, many of them the same words.

It was an odd business and a strange way to earn money, but maybe the oddest thing was that it stopped feeling odd after a while. And, no, I never did expect it to go on forever. It just sometimes seemed like it might.

So while my work life was disappearing like mist under a new sun, our world was changing in other ways, too. It seemed to have lost a little of its zing, though I failed to notice at first, or I just didn't want to see it.

The move to Wellington wasn't working out, not at all, not at first anyway. In the face of the alien weather, overwhelming homesickness for balmy abandoned Auckland, and a strange new life in a strange new place, it was a struggle adjusting. We all suffered various forms of shock, often requiring medication, even psychological intervention.

And, if all that wasn't quite enough, there seemed to be constant reminders of mortality, not all of them to do with me finding myself, quite suddenly it seemed, in my mid-sixties, something I'd never really envisioned being. No, it wasn't only about me.

Only a few months after we'd moved, Philippa's father, Keith, died. He was a man with a large, warm presence and I was very fond of him. I was also in his debt.

All those years ago, despite the fact that I had five kids and I was 16 years older than his beautiful daughter, he had welcomed me into the family.

We got on easily, too. I could make him laugh, and he was a font of good, down-to-earth advice. We'd sit out on his veranda in Gisborne when we went to visit him and Philippa's mum, Shirley, in later years. I'd roll him cigarettes because his old hands were too fumbly and useless to do that anymore, and give him a bit of cheek and listen to his stories.

His life had become pretty miserable, but he never lost his spirit or his joy in the company of others. When the pain started biting really deeply, and it seemed he should try whatever was necessary to push it back, some of us encouraged him to try smoking a little marijuana, which he did. He reckoned it made him feel a bit better, though Shirley said it also made him talk too much and want more pudding than was good for him.

Keith was very solid on practical matters. 'Don't ever buy a chainsaw, Col,' he said when I mentioned I might, and I listened. He knew I was a useless city softie and I'd probably cut my foot off. Every time I saw him I made a point of thanking him for letting me have his lovely daughter and he laughed.

But he was 82 by then, and, although he was an old farmer and a tough bugger, he'd been ill for years and it was all too much for him in the end. And while death delivered him from his pain, it was a hard loss and it really hit Philippa. They were very close. It hit all of us in ways death does that you can never anticipate.

And then Sheryl, Gordon's ex-wife, the girl who tried to get me dates way back in Invercargill, the mother of Gordon's and her now-grown-up daughter and the grandmother of their grandchildren, died suddenly.

She was only as old as Gordon and I. That seemed shocking. And, by cruel coincidence, Sheryl died on the same day as Gordon's wife Patricia's brother died from the cancer he'd been suffering. Gordon and Patricia drove to the East Coast to see him in his last moments and, shortly after, Gordie got the news about Sheryl.

And then, only a little later, my own father, who had just reluctantly turned 91, went into what would be his final decline, refusing food and medicine in the end, not wanting to be here anymore. 'It is what it is' was about the last thing he said to me before he turned altogether silent.

But it was what it was, as Dad said, perhaps stumbling on the meaning of life itself.

So I decided the best and possibly the only way to cope was to steadfastly refuse to see a pattern in any of these things, not even after Gordon told me about his health issue. I decided to defer to my inner hippie for the purposes of comfort and ongoingness.

Life really seems happiest if it can remain full of possibilities. Not endless possibilities, but quite a number of them. Every moment holds at least one of them, and they're best when they're joined together.

Which must be where the road trip came in.

# MONDAY

Six days would do it, we thought. We'd fly into and out of Queenstown, pick up a big fat rental car and drive what we called the loop, down Lake Wakatipu to Kingston and out across Southland, then up through Otago to Dunedin, and west across the high country back to Queenstown and out again. To further cement arrangements, we booked hotels in Invercargill, Dunedin and Naseby.

At Wellington Airport, Gordie announces, 'Fuck, I forgot to bring a book', pops into the book shop and buys Neil Young's memoir *Waging Heavy Peace*. It's patchy and slightly crazy, I tell him, but then so are Neil's albums these days. And Neil himself is slightly crazy. I interviewed him a couple of times, years back. Once, I spent the best part of a day with him when he was in Auckland for a concert. I have a photo of him windsurfing on the Waitemata, which seemed an unlikely thing for Neil Young to do.

Gordie seems in good spirits, but then Gordie always seems in good spirits. 'I'm looking forward to this jaunt,' he says, plopping back into a seat in the Koru lounge, opening

Neil. It's going to be interesting, six days and nights together on this trip back to I'm not sure what. It's got me thinking of that Bob Dylan song 'Mississippi' with the line that goes, 'You can always come back, but you can't come back all the way'. And then there's that other thing Bob said about nostalgia being death, but I'm not sure he really meant that.

Gordie and I have strangely similar hand-written letters we sent, unknown to each other, as schoolboys looking for jobs as reporters at *The Southland Times*. That, as mentioned, was 46 years ago, and, though we've known each other, off and on, all this time, I'm not sure how well we really know each other at all.

The flight to Queenstown has been delayed, but that hardly seems to matter when we're going back in time anyway. The plane's flying late because it was hit by lightning coming in, someone says. I ring my mother in Christchurch, 'just to say bye before we fly', I tell her, not mentioning the lightning.

She's 88 and persistent in her beliefs, even when they're off the mark. 'You and Gordon went to school together, of course,' she tells me. 'No, Mum,' I tell her. 'We met each other later. We worked and flatted together.' But she's not having any of that. 'You were at high school together and then the newspaper,' she says. I consider protesting, but give up. Gordie's mother is also 88 and a little less old-fashioned than mine. He tells me she's recently bought a new car and an iPad.

We're finally seated on our plane, and madly affable Gordie is chatting to the bloke in the next seat. The stranger lives in Queenstown. It's six degrees there today, according to the pilot. Gordie and his new pal start talking about the winds in Wellington. The southerly change gets its inevitable name-check. Gordie's telling the stranger we're off on a road trip. I hear my friend refer to me as 'an old rock-and-roller'.

'Car or bikes?' the stranger asks.

'Bikes?' I yelp from my seat. He must think we're a couple of gay old ganders off to pedal the rail trail.

'Harleys I meant,' says the stranger consolingly from his window seat. I decide it's best to ignore him.

Down our plane lazily drifts between mountains and, bonk, we're here, with Queenstown a sudden great big eyeful as we step out into it — sun, mountains, gorse blooming, aquamarine river and lake, of course. Looking like a postcard, as always.

By prior agreement, and because neither of us likes it much, we skip Queenstown, the town itself, altogether, and drive straight south down the lake, misty mountaintops on both sides. We stop at the café that sits on the turn-off to Kingston, where the lake ends. We fancy cheese rolls and coffee.

I pulled in here a few years back and, behaving like the Aucklander I was then, ordered my flat white double strength. 'It's already double strength,' the young man behind the counter protested. But I didn't trust his rural double strength of course, and insisted that he double his double, which he duly did and brought it to me with a little smile on his face. Then he watched me quietly from across the café as I tried to cope with the strongest coffee

I've ever encountered. I flew from the place, legs trembling, head buzzing.

'Where does Southland start exactly?' I ask the young barista, who shows no signs of remembering me, though he may not be the same young barista as last time. After a while all young baristas look alike, and, doubtless, it's hard to keep a good coffee-maker in quiet Kingston, permanent population 30-odd. Quite odd, possibly. Staring up that great endless lake all day might bend anyone's outlook.

'Just down the road,' says the young barista. 'There's a sign.'

The cheese rolls are excellent, Gordie and I agree, even with the crusts left on, which had brought a raised eyebrow from my travelling companion, who, it'll turn out, has high standards when it comes to food. 'We're proud of our

cheese rolls,' the young man says. Gordie takes a photo of them with his phone. He might tweet it, he says.

'You tweet?' I ask him.

'Well, I started a few years back, then I stopped, but I thought I might start again on this trip.'

'How many followers have you got?'

'Seventeen or so.'

'Or so?'

It was Gordie who organised our rental car, a nice big blue Falcon. Not too blue. Not pastel blue, thank God. Once, on a trip down here, I got stuck with a bright yellow rental. A compact. It was an embarrassment. I felt like I was travelling around in a buttercup. You don't want a brightly coloured car in these parts. The locals might think we're metrosexuals.

Gordie's going to be doing the driving. I've been assured by people I trust that he's steady and reasonably safe behind the wheel, and anyway I need him to drive so I can take notes in case I end up writing something about all this.

Seeing me breaking out the stationery, he recalls the time he was out on the road reporting and had to write a story as he drove back from somewhere or other, pad propped on the steering wheel, scribbling, chasing the deadline. I used to think deadlines were the only thing that kept us honest.

We drive down from the café into Kingston town, which is more a village really, slumberous and unbothered by the millionaire mansions that surround that ever-spreading, over-priced Aspen of the south, Queenstown.

Several Kingston cribs near the edge of the great lapping lake are for sale. The downside of this little miracle of a place is the great cliff of the mountains going up forever between Kingston and the afternoon sun. That and the lake, which is tidal and invades the village when the mood takes it.

According to Maori legend, the rapid tidal movement that is so odd and individual to Lake Wakatipu isn't tidal at all and nothing to do with the moon or any of that. Instead, the waters are being moved by the still-beating heart of a giant called Matua, who lived in the mountains around here back in the times when giants walked the land.

Matua was a bad bugger who stole a beautiful human girl and took her back to his lair. But before the monster could figure out how to progress the relationship, the young woman's lover came to her rescue, setting fire to the great bed of ferns Matua was sleeping on and suffocating the giant with the smoke.

In his death agonies, so the rather graphic legend goes, Matua drew up his knees, and the fire, made fierce now by his burning body fat, roared red to the skies and sank him deep into the earth, forming the bed of the lake, which promptly filled with water from the melted snows.

Glenorchy, at the far top of the northern reach of the lake, is the giant's head, Queenstown his bent knees, Kingston his feet. And, way down below the waters, Matua's angry heart beats still, explaining the tides. It makes sense. There are other theories about the lake and its twitchy tide, but they're a great deal less interesting.

As promised by the barista, a little way from Kingston down Highway 6 to Invercargill we find the Southland District sign. *People First* it declares. It's made of stiff steel.

There are four bullet punches in it — fired from the Otago side, judging by the angle.

On we roll, down through Garston, then Athol, neither of them even towns at all anymore. They favour funny names in these parts. We stop at a long-abandoned old shop that catches our gaze, just off the road. Its sign is nearly weathered completely away. Fisherman's Rest it was called the last time it was in business, though you won't know even that in a few years.

This place, which hardly seems a place at all now, is called Parawa. There's another nearly-gone sign, this one for a long-ago southern ice-cream brand we both remember, Manda. The abandoned tearoom started life way back in 1867 as the Parawa Junction Hotel, taking care of passing travellers. The little town that used to be here peaked around 1904 when the local flax mill employed 20 men,

who would have lived with their families around the area. Now there's no one and nothing except an old pub waiting to fall down.

On down the road, Lumsden, the 'Hub of North Southland', is quiet, with several cafés present but not open for business. A newspaper reporter wrote of this place nearly a century ago, 'There is not a great deal of Lumsden, nor is it a particularly wide-awake centre. At the present rate of progress, Lumsden will have a thousand inhabitants by 1950 and may then achieve the dignity of a municipal borough.'

As things turned out, that dignity never quite came. The population is now only a few hundred and quietly falling.

This is where we start to feel the tilt of the plains. It's all a gentle ride downhill from here, all the way to Invercargill. We stop at the dairy at Dipton, home of

Deputy Prime Minister Bill English and not many others. We need cigarettes and cigarette papers.

There's not a Dipton resident in sight, but there must be someone behind the shop counter. I can hear Gordie shouting cheerful things at whoever's in there, wanting to know what the vibe is in Dipton, whether Bill's ever about these days, the weather forecast.

And here comes Gordie and on we drive, Warren Zevon on the car stereo up loud, singing 'that dead man song' of his, making me want to turn it off because it makes me sad about my friend who's sitting here next to me, smiling at the road ahead like everything's alright, which it is, in this moment.

But I've only just connected with him properly again, and he's apparently going to be taken away in the not-far-off future. I'm not feeling very happy about this. I am quite angry with God, who I never much counted on anyway. In fact, I'm starting to suspect that God might have it in for us baby-boomers for all our wicked waywardness, our self-indulgence and our extremely poor church attendance.

Winton welcomes us with its sizeable cemetery, which sits to the left on an attractive rise at the northern outskirts of town. Winton, population around 2000, is looking quite lively and fully occupied. It's the town that sucked up the other littler towns out here across the plains north and west of Invercargill, Southland's big sprawling capital city.

Apart from being still remembered as the hometown of a famous child murderer, Winton was for a while also famous for quite a foolish thing, its wooden railway line, though there's little trace of it now and even less talk.

With the gold rush booming just over the line in Otago in the 1860s, Invercargill was the nearest port for the supply of over-priced comestibles to those rich miners. But the problem was that, south of Winton as the land sank towards sea level, the road turned into a treacherous bog for much of the year, offering very gooey going for the wagons and their big teams of bullocks.

Not wanting the mere matter of mud to stop the region from getting its share of the gold, the newly formed Southland Provincial Council decided to build a railway line across the 30-odd kilometres from Invercargill to Winton, from where the road continued, nice and dry across the higher and well-drained part of the Southland Plains.

But then, hoping to save some money in the process, the council opted to use rail lines made of wood instead of the usual steel. They figured they could have them made for next to nothing from the nice native trees in the nearby forests. After all, there had been wooden railways constructed in other parts of the world, like England and

Malaya, though they had a tendency to catch fire, it was said, and the one in Malaya was eaten by termites.

So the Southland Provincial Council started chopping trees down and had their line laid 10 kilometres out of town before they decided to pull the plug on the mad scheme. They'd discovered that among the many drawbacks of wooden railways was the fact that the train's wheels had a tendency to spin if the rails were wet, which, being in Southland, they very often were. Even when it did run, the train was so slow that the locals could walk faster, something they enjoyed demonstrating to their foolish leaders.

By the time the cheapskate council admitted their mistake and replaced the line with expensive iron rails, it was 1870 and the Central Otago gold rush was pretty much done and dusted. Then, when the Government funded the continuation of the railway all the way through to Kingston, half of Winton went with it and never came home, leaving the town to struggle on towards the twentieth century.

But Winton seems fine and fully open for business these days. There's a prosperous air about the place. I wind down the window to sniff it. We don't stop, though. We can feel the pull of Invercargill.

And, merely 20 minutes down the road, here it comes, looming up on us, though it's a geographical challenge for a pancake-flat place to actually loom very effectively. Invercargill, more accurately, forms around us as we cruise in, down the endless and relentlessly straight approach from the north, the North Road, which is grandly, madly wide from some long-ago self-belief.

And here we are in the unbustling heart of the city, turning into Kelvin Street, parking right outside and checking into the Kelvin Hotel, where we've booked two rooms for three nights.

That's a long time in Invercargill, we'd agreed, but there's a lot of exploring to be done in Southland, and it was best, we decided, to have a base fully equipped with the essentials of life — a house bar, a restaurant and a smoking balcony, which the Kelvin has (there's one on every floor).

But we barely have time to drop our bags and catch a breath, because we're starting the journey into the past immediately with a visit to *The Southland Times*. Before we left home in Wellington, Gordie had tracked down the current editor of the paper and emailed him to make an appointment for us to visit. The *Times* office is right where we left it, in its old building in Esk Street, just around the corner from the Kelvin. The acting editor, Mark, who might be 40 or so, greets us for what turns out to be a sad sort of tour. If there are any past glories here, then they're hidden.

The lift's the same, a tiny metal coffin, slow and creaking. This is the lift an unaccompanied goat walked out of onto the editorial floor late one night, wandering over and eating a couple of the stories sitting in my out tray.

Another night, the lift door opened and a man pedalled out on his bike. He was the town's most prominent crazy person, a Christian by the name of Arnold Brooker, who had a model church he'd put together sitting on his bicycle carrier. He rode once around Mr Grimaldi's office before catching the lift back down. That lift could tell a lot of stories.

And they might be cheerier than Mark's tales of woe. He tells us he's only the acting and not the deputy editor, when we accidentally call him that, because they, the group that owns the paper now, don't believe in deputy editors. They do still have an editor, who's out of town, and then there's a tier of people who could be acting editor. Today it's Mark's turn.

There used to be 300 people working at *The Southland Times*, he tells us, but now there are only 50-odd, rattling around in this cavernous old place, which the remaining staff might be moving out of shortly.

The only thing Gordie and I remember from the old days really is the lift.

Well, that and the old court drawings of Southland's most famous murderer, Minnie Dean, which are on a wall, which might be where Mr Grimaldi's office once was, but it's hard to tell because it's a shared work station now and it's missing a wall. I recall it used to have an open fire burning coal, keeping all those old editors warm down the years.

When I joined *The Southland Times*, the Reporters' Room, as it was called, was not notable for the artworks hanging on its fag-stained walls. But there was that one thing looking down on us, Minnie in her frame.

Born, as mentioned, up the road in Winton, she was hanged only a short walk from the newspaper office in the late 1880s for the murders of a number of babies put in her care. It was said that she put hat needles through their fontanelles to kill them. The number was never agreed on, but it could have been as many as 20. They were unwanted babies and the records weren't well kept. Dean was spotted when a sharp-eyed conductor saw her getting on the train for Lumsden with a baby and a hatbox, and getting off with just the hatbox.

Minnie Dean was the only woman ever to be hanged in New Zealand. According to *The Southland Times* of the time, 'She walked firmly and erectly to the scaffold without fear or distress, her last words a brief prayer that she might not suffer. She died instantly. She was 47.' In the court drawing she looked much older than 47, a tiny chinless woman in a strange little black bonnet.

A curious local watching the hanging from a nearby roof slipped and fell to the street below, breaking some bones. It was the sight of the hangman swinging from Dean's legs to be sure her neck was good and snapped that made him lose his hold, others sitting nearby reported.

Minnie Dean was buried by her husband, Charles, in an unmarked grave out at that old cemetery on the northern outskirts of Winton. Her resting place can be found by entering the Winton Cemetery through the second entrance. Dean's plot is the last on the left, opposite James and John Spowart. Even in death she remains the single most interesting thing about Winton, apart from my first wife, who was born in the town.

Gordie chats enthusiastically to everyone we run into on our visit to *The Southland Times*, though there are few of them left working in the place now. There are quite a few desks in the Reporters' Room, but they're what they call 'hot desks', meaning they're shared work stations. Only a few reporters are even around.

One of them is a new recruit finishing her first day with *The Southland Times*. She's written a couple of stories, she says. 'It'll be the first day of the rest of your life tomorrow,' I tell her, trying not to sound like an old dork, 'seeing your first stories in print'. She smiles nervously. I have several daughters older than her. I feel utterly ancient and suddenly very thirsty.

'Let's get out of here,' I whisper to Gordie as Mark the acting editor leads us towards another empty room that used to be something else. He's not very hopeful about the future, he says. It's all too bloody depressing.

When Gordie and I started at the paper several generations ago, the atmosphere was anything but depressing. Apart from anything else, the atmosphere was full of smoke. Then, everyone smoked cigarettes like their lives depended on it. Wastepaper baskets would burst into flames occasionally from discarded matches. We were so busy we barely noticed.

Alcohol loomed large in lifestyle and blood. Everything loomed large. There was a guy working at the paper, the first man I ever heard say 'The fucking fucker's fucked' about something or other that was, obviously, quite fucked. He might have been referring to his hand of poker. We used to play poker with the printers sometimes after work.

There were a couple of senior writers at the *Times* who were so senior that they still wrote their copy by hand with fountain pens, never having adapted to ballpoints, never mind typewriters.

One of them, FWG (Fred) Miller, wrote poems under the byline 'The Poet'. They were sponsored by one of the big local bakeries, and ran in a little box on the front page of the paper each morning from the 1940s right through until the 1970s.

They weren't Yeats. They were more Wordsworth, though less florid and shorter, of course. Often they addressed the weather, but not always. Usually they were humorous. It's been estimated that Fred wrote more than 10,000 poems in that time. Like this one, which apparently upset some Southlanders, who to this very day tend to be sensitive about their climate.

*The clouds at long last broke apart*
*The old man gave a sigh*
*As to his awed, delighted gaze*
*An orb shone in the sky —*
*A bright, resplendent, radiant thing*
*That hovered for an hour,*
*And once again slid modestly*
*Behind another shower.*

*'Hurrah, hurrah,' the old man said,*
*'that thing must be the sun.*
*I had to see before I died*
*And now my day is done!*
*So that's the sun, so that's the sun,'*
*He said as down he sat,*
*'Often in my boyhood days*
*My father spoke of that!'*

Fred Miller was a lovely old guy, a long-time member of the Invercargill Licensing Trust, and a man with a finely honed instinct for a free drink and a slight air of the old movie comedian WC Fields about him, though much less rambunctious and a great deal fonder of children and gardening. He was whimsical and had some great lines, like his philosophy for life, which went: 'Pain is inevitable, misery is optional. Stick a geranium in your hat and be happy.'

What a place that newspaper was, such an odd other-world. Working there was a bit like joining the circus without having to run away, though of course you never quite got back to the real world after newspapers, and you never saw the real world the same way again once you were taught to question everything.

In those days, a cadet reporter started out at the very bottom and worked his or her way up from there, did the dirty work, fetched pies from the pie cart for the subs at supper time, picked up packages from the railway, took down the sports results over the phone, walked around and got the shipping movements from the shipping office.

And even when you did get to go out posing as a proper reporter, the most interesting thing you might get to do for a while was the hotel round, which involved visiting Invercargill's handful of downtown hotels and asking to see the guest books, in the usually vain hope there might be someone interesting staying.

And by interesting I mean that the guest was from somewhere interesting, somewhere overseas maybe. Then you'd request an interview, inquire of the foreign visitor what brought them to Invercargill and what, if anything, had caught their fancy about the place. Well, maybe I used to ask that because I was beginning to wonder myself.

Or perhaps you simply took fright at all this strangeness and the other-worldly hours and the fags and the booze and dropped out of the newspaper life altogether to do something less life-altering, like school teaching or lion taming. Being a scribbler wasn't for everyone.

The chief reporter when I joined *The Southland Times* was a man called Grant Graham, and his deputy was Garth George, both of them labelled with two first names, the same initials, and both of them a handful, but in completely contrasting ways. Grant Graham was a flinty, humourless type, oddly suspicious of any reporter who wanted to actually leave the office in search of a story.

Garth George, on the other handful, was notable mainly for his absences from the office. He liked a drink and he also liked the ladies, and could often be found leaning on a bar in one of the nearby hotels, like Deschler's, which was across the road from the paper and down Esk Street a few steps. Or maybe the Cecil, around the corner and up some stairs, more like an old speakeasy than a hotel. Both are gone now.

One of my early assignments was to track Garth down and try to pry him from his drink and barmaid and get him back to work. 'Fuck off, Hogg,' he said.

'I couldn't find him, Mr Graham,' I reported back to the chief reporter, who, while he didn't swear, could be very unpleasant and didn't seem to enjoy his job at all. Another young reporter, Janet Finlay I think her name was, became so maddened by our boss's bloody-mindedness over something that one evening she leapt from her desk, screamed an awful accusation and threw her typewriter at him, missing by some distance, but making a spectacular noise and severely damaging her instrument. Then she ran off to the shelter of the Lady Editor's Office, where she knew no man would follow.

We had to buy our own typewriters in those days. I arrived at the *Times* armed with a brand-new Olivetti Lettera 32, a snappy, blue-green metal portable that I hammered for 20 years before bending it badly at the end of the 1980s when I threw it at a wall in Noumea, where I was on the road in trying circumstances with the band Herbs.

Apart from buying our own typewriters, we were also supposed to arrange shorthand and touch-typing lessons at our own expense, but I couldn't find time for either and, like many newspaper reporters then, I developed my own versions of both.

This could be a testing situation in my early days, especially on Sundays when I'd be on the phone half the night hopelessly trying to type down golf results from various country correspondents. They were usually half drunk and eager to get the job done and head back to the nineteenth hole for another gin. They'd get angry with me. Very angry. And sweary. I recall a lot of yelling in the early days.

'Call this an intro, Hogg?' That would be the chief sub, a small, fierce, bright-eyed man called Jim Valli. The Subs' Room was through a double-hinged door from the Reporters' Room. There was plenty of space above and below the swinging door for the yelling to come through. It was best to learn what you were supposed to be doing fairly quickly, if only to stop all the yelling.

There were other tribes we journalists-in-the-making co-existed with at the newspaper. There were the printers, rugged, inky-fingered, union-loving characters in coats and aprons. The printer in charge wore a tie. They liked a laugh, especially if it was at the expense of one of us scribblers. One night at the *Times* one of them sidled up to me and inquired if I wanted to buy a ticket in their raffle. 'What's the prize?' I asked. After all, I didn't want to look like a fool.

'Six bottles of piss,' he said. 'Piss', in the rough parlance of the time, meant beer. Well, that's what I thought. Then, before I knew it, I'd had the great fortune to win the printers' raffle and went out to pick up my prize to great roars of laughter in the compositing room as I was handed a crate with six milk bottles filled, to varying levels, with piss alright. It was printers' piss. It turned out that they all had to submit regular urine samples to have checks made on their lead levels, given that they handled so much of the metal.

And then there were the readers, who had their own room, too, and sat there, like a cast straight out of Charles Dickens, reading and checking for mistakes in our stories. They were next to the Subs' Room, connected by a hatch-sized opening with a glass slide. There was no love lost between those rooms. No one liked the readers much, a bunch of odd chooks who today no longer even exist in newspapers, killed off by spell-check.

The readers at *The Southland Times* were mostly women, though the head reader was a man, a pedantic old bugger called Hec Marshall, who was forever getting up our noses with his know-all, finger-pointing, glasses-on-the-end-of-his-snorer ways. This occasionally drove us to play cruel tricks on him.

There was the night we hooked up a big dead rat by its tail to the spring-loaded flying fox device that shot copy back and forth from the printers through to the Readers' Room and fired that fat rat straight through to Hec and his chooks. And the night when we went way out over the mark, typing up a fake story about the Queen being assassinated in Australia, in the midst of Her Majesty's then-current tour of the colonies. We watched through the glass partition as old Hec, a vociferous royalist, rose to his feet, white-faced and trembling, to announce the awful news to his staff. One of the ladies fainted. I don't recall how we resolved that awful prank or if I was ever really forgiven.

Out the back from editorial were the various printing departments: the compositors, then the linotype operators with their jittering steam-punk machines full of molten lead. And, down below in the bowels, the pressroom, which would come alive after the witching hour, pumping out thousands of papers for letterboxes all over the province. What a sweet and wonderful time it was, but so long ago.

After some confusion with getting back out onto Esk Street through the newspaper's unpredictable self-locking doors, we manage to escape from what's left of *The Southland Times* and swiftly get ourselves into a bar a few steps around the corner on the ground floor of the Kelvin.

There used to be a straight-off-the-street bar right on the corner at the Kelvin. It was called, with good Southland logic, the Corner Bar, and it was very popular with the *Times* journos, especially around five when they put the cheese and biscuits out on the bar. But the Corner Bar's gone and there's a new bar called the Editor's Cut. 'What the fuck,' ponders Gordon loudly, 'is an editor's cut?'

'Someone probably thought it sounded good, without checking if it actually meant anything first, which it doesn't, unless it's some sort of old pipe tobacco,' I venture.

The Farm Editor at *The Southland Times* smoked a pipe, constantly as I recall. You took your life in your hands getting in that little lift with him. I think his name was Norman, though us young pups had to call him 'Mister'.

Under the influence of a couple of drinks, Gordie admits that it was he who put Arnold the mad Christian in the *Southland Times* lift that night and gave him directions for his historic ride around the Editor's Office. He can't remember why he did it.

Arnold was a persistent character about Invercargill at the time, a challenging and brighter-than-usual sort of village idiot. He had even done some time in psychiatric care for his intense beliefs.

He had a certificate of some sort that they'd given him when he was released, attesting to his sanity, and he'd pull it out and wave it under the nose of anyone who had the cheek to tell him he was mad. 'Where's yours?' he'd ask.

Arnold would also cycle the city in the early hours and write the word 'Invictus' on lamp posts and empty milk bottles that caught his eye. Often the *Southland Times* milk bottles suffered his attentions. Arnold was a pioneer tagger and, like many of the taggers of today, it wasn't entirely clear what he was saying, though he might have been referring to a poem titled 'Invictus', written in 1887 by an Englishman, William Ernest Henley, which, in part, goes:

> *Out of the night that covers me,*
> *Black as the pit from pole to pole,*
> *I thank whatever gods may be*
> *For my unconquerable soul.*
>
> *In the fell clutch of circumstance*
> *I have not winced nor cried aloud.*
> *Under the bludgeonings of chance*
> *My head is bloody, but unbowed.*

Not that I ever heard of Arnold Brooker's head being bludgeoned bloody, and I'm sure it wasn't. Invercargill wasn't exactly a soft spot to call home in those days, but nor was it harsh and violent, unless you happened to be a sheep or perhaps a young chap with long hair.

Arnold eventually moved on to spread his mad message up the country, and spent his later years living in central Wellington pursuing what he now referred to as his prophetic ministry, still carting his model church about, along with a jester's cap and a blanket with Jesus embroidered on it that he wore as a cape.

He died in 2004 in the capital, a beloved and even celebrated local eccentric, aged 93. The singer Mahinarangi Tocker wrote a song called 'Arnold Brooker' about him, and there's even a documentary film called *The Whirling*

*Man* dedicated to him. Being crazy sometimes works out quite well for people in New Zealand.

I'm not entirely sure why Arnold left Invercargill, but one day he wasn't there anymore and the city's milk bottles were safe. Maybe he just needed more attention.

It has always been difficult to attract much attention from Southland, New Zealand's furthest-away, most-misunderstood, least-known and perhaps least-loved place. Even worse, people from other parts of the country sometimes take the piss. You find this stuff out only after you leave, and it has the unsettling effect of sometimes making you feel protective about a place you once couldn't wait to get out of.

But generally outsiders are silly about Southland. Bluff oysters, blue cod and tender spring legs of lamb aside, the local diet is often portrayed as being remarkable for its inclusion of the swede turnip. And the locals, perhaps as a result of heavy ingestion of said swede, speak with a disturbing emphasis on the letter 'r', as in 'Inverrrrcarrrrgill', or indeed 'Rrriverrrton' or 'Rrriverrrsdale', along with several other place names in Southland riddled with rrrs, like 'Gorrre'.

Gordie takes some pride in the fact that, even though he grew up in the absolute backblocks of Southland where that telltale accent looms largest, he doesn't roll his 'r's when he speaks. To my ear, he has adopted a slightly posh lilt, though I'd assumed that it was his years as a TV reporter that dealt to his diction.

My speech is not marked by the letter 'r' either, but I didn't move to Invercargill until I was eight, and I'd grown up, anyway, with a Scottish accent from my Scottish immigrant parents and grandparents, something I'd only just shaken off.

But I had no issues about moving to Invercargill, not that I had any choice. When I was a kid growing up there in the late 1950s and the 1960s, it seemed as big a place as anyone could ever possibly need.

There were three movie houses, the Civic Theatre (where The Rolling Stones and The Pretty Things played), the hiss of coffee bars, and even a level of bright lights that made the city's downtown streets glow and glitter if you squinted your eyes a bit and held your head a certain way. It looked better in the rain, and that was a good thing because the rain was always readily available.

The barmaid behind the bar in the Editor's Cut is Allie, according to her name tag, and she's phenomenally friendly, almost unseemly with her torrent of 'lovies', 'dearies' and even a passing 'darl' or two. It's her version of southern warmth, I suppose. But it's gone six o'clock now and Allie's winning ways won't keep us here.

We head upstairs to the first-floor house bar for another beer, and then dinner, after a bit, in the hotel restaurant, an old-fashioned place with lots of meat on the menu.

The rack of lamb is local, of course, and sensitively cooked, though there's a bit too much happening elsewhere on the plate. The 'apricot pillows', we agree, are a culinary step too far, strange little fruit-filled pastry things.

On impulse, possibly excited to be away on our first night, we order Irish coffees and then head up to the fourth-floor smoking balcony, Gordie for a ciggie, me for a few puffs on my particular drug, which has long been a social problem, but that's never put me off.

Gordie, on the other hand, has just started smoking cigarettes again off the back of his bad news. 'Might as well' is his attitude. He's eating and drinking what he feels like, too.

Out on the smoking balcony, we're looking right across Kelvin Street to the H&J Smith department store electronic clock and temperature tower, with the city's famous water tower set nicely, a kilometre or two distant, to its left. It's got to be one of the best views in town, though that's not saying an awful lot in Invercargill, where there aren't a lot of views to be had.

After my dad had been promoted to head office in Christchurch, he would visit Invercargill every month or two for work purposes and stay here at the Kelvin Hotel. Rather than cause alarm by visiting me at my decrepit flat, he'd invite me to dinner at the hotel and take me into the house bar for a drink first, which I thought was pretty sophisticated.

I don't know what we talked about, but the Kelvin Hotel was where my grown-up relationship with my father started, in a quite formal way. I think I used to even put a tie on for him.

Gordie interviewed the future famous Australian prime minister Bob Hawke in the Kelvin once. Bob was president of the ACTU at the time. It's one of Gordie's key interview memories. The rugged and straight-talking union boss was in Invercargill for lord-knows-what reason and staying at the hotel. He invited Gordon up to his executive suite to do the interview. 'He had Steinlager,' says Gordie. 'It was the first time I'd ever drunk Steinlager. I think it had recently come on the market.' I think it's really the beer Gordie remembers the interview for more than the man.

Back in my room, number 404 on the fourth floor, there's a view off over the roofs to the endless flatness and the sun that doesn't seem to want to set. It's past ten o'clock and the sky is filled with light.

Hours ago, as we were drifting down from Otago into Southland, Gordie looked over his steering wheel at the big plains ahead and said, 'I've always felt ambivalent about this place.'

I went through years of really not liking Invercargill much at all, but I've come around to it a little in recent times. My mother always liked the place, and still insists she was sad to leave and move to Christchurch. To this day, she talks about how she wouldn't mind moving back, though she won't now, being 88 and all set up in a nice retirement village.

I don't know how Dad felt about Invercargill. I don't think he had a particular affection for any one place, or even several. Perhaps that's a mark of his life experience. Perhaps it's because he put so much effort into getting away from the place he grew up in. I believe that's what makes him and Mum a little like those immigrants nearly a hundred years before them who fled Scotland and the lot they'd been cast to find a new life in just about the furthest-away place on the planet.

But though New Zealand was far away, the parts of the new country the Scots chose to resettle themselves in weren't entirely unfamiliar. The challenging climate and landscape of the parts of Southland and Otago in which they chose to put down their hardy new roots were a lot like what they came from.

I've been to Edinburgh. I've felt that wind, that icy edge, and I grew up feeling it in the mad hills of Dunedin and the madder flatness of Invercargill. All that was different were the people, except that there were already a lot of Scottish people living in the nether regions of New Zealand by the time Mum and Dad arrived.

Dad left behind five sisters he loved and a mother he adored to come with his new family to New Zealand. He never said whether that hurt. He never talked much about that, his life that is. But in recent years, as I saw him starting to fade, I got into the habit, when I visited him and Mum in Christchurch, of quietly interviewing him about his life, starting from the earliest stuff he could remember.

After I had built up a pad full of notes over a few visits, I wrote his story up. I kept it in the first person, but I jazzed it up a bit, trying to catch his voice and let him put his side of the story. At home, we never got to hear his side of the story.

## A FATHER'S STORY

I grew up in unusual circumstances in the 1920s and 1930s in southern Scotland. They call the region the Borders. It's only 40 miles from old, crowded Edinburgh, but a world away really.

My father was the centre of it all, I realised, as soon as I properly began to realise things. He was big, but the biggest things about him were his hands. He'd gone to Canada in his teens and worked as a lumberjack in the endless forests there.

I was born in Galashiels in 1923. We lived at 176 Scott Street. As to what my father, Harold, did for a job, a nice name for it would be 'general dealer'. He bought and sold things. Starting out in his self-made business, he sold waste from the woollen mills in Galashiels, which was full of woollen mills then. It was what made Galashiels the lively town it was.

My father had previously had a business as a woodcutter, chopping down trees on the big estates that surrounded the town. He sold the wood on, for building and for the grate.

There were six or seven mills in Gala, and dye works as well. They were all built there for the power of the river. The workers were mostly women on the machines, with the men doing maintenance, but it was mostly women. Galashiels was a town of about 12- or 14,000 people. It was a working-class town with big families. I had a friend who was one of 18. I didn't know any other world. I didn't see the ocean until I was 18; on the same day I saw Edinburgh for the first time. I'd thought Gala was as big as it got.

My mother Elizabeth's father was what they called a 'grieve'. He worked on one of the big estates owned by some duke or other. Grieves were like foremen, controlling the workers on the estate. Grieves got a better class of cottage.

In Gala we rented a three-storey house in a terrace. The top storey was the attic, a big bedroom for all the kids. I had five sisters.

When I was about 14 we moved to Gattonside and a country sort of life only a few miles from Gala. 'Gatton' means garden in the old language, and Gattonside was across the river from the old abbey at Melrose. It was hardly even a village when we lived there, and it was still filled with trees from the old orchards the monks had kept.

Our new house was so big I had my own room. It was an old farmhouse with 40 fruit trees, russet apples, pears, peaches. My father had electricity and sewerage put in early on. He always had money. Then he had a bad crash in one of his big cars and was in bed for months. I was 12 and he took me out of school to keep an eye on things for him.

The mills were starting to close. He bought one, broke up the machinery and sold it for scrap. He must have made a profit, because he bought more. He had teams of men working for him. They were rough types. He put me in charge of a mill he bought in a town called Peebles. I was 14. It was a hard way to learn about human nature.

My father lived well, but there was less for us. Mum was given 30 shillings a week to feed everyone. She'd run out of money every week, but never say anything to him. My father always had a car. He had a gift for making money. He was an intelligent man who strayed to the bent side. He could be violent.

As part of his varied business interests, he also dealt with poachers, who brought him mostly rabbits, which they caught in traps, and salmon. Another way to catch rabbits, if you came across a mass of burrows, was to send ferrets down to bring them out so that you could catch them in nets like fish. I remember hearing the ground thunder as they came to the surface in terror of the ferrets.

There was still a lot of old forest around, mostly on the estates. One of the forests was said to be haunted by a legion of Roman soldiers who'd been sent north from Hadrian's Wall to punish some of our wild ancestors, never to be seen again. Except by drunks weaving home along lonely roads on moonlit nights.

Then the war came along and swept me up. In the Army I was somebody. I didn't want to go back to the village. I seemed to thrive in the uniform. I rose to sergeant and, because of my natural skills with a gun and my outdoor ways, I was put into what they called later the Secret Army.

We were trained in resistance-style fighting. We were to become the underground army when the Germans invaded. They were saying 'when' and not 'if', at the time. So I passed the war mostly in Scotland, and I stayed on in the Army after the war ended and started thinking about what to do.

Going off to another country seemed a good idea. I had been planning to go alone, though I hadn't taken any action beyond thinking about it.

I met Mary in July 1947, and left the Army at the end of that year. I had thought to stay on, but the Army became soft after the war. It wasn't the sort of Army I wanted anymore and, anyway, there was Mary.

She was dark, tall, with big eyes I could feel looking inside me like no one ever had. I met her at a dance I'd gone to when I was out on the town in Edinburgh one Saturday night with some other Army sergeants.

I couldn't dance, but I'd drunk enough that night to be mad enough to try. Mary noticed me, she said later, when I tripped over and fell on the dance floor trying to steer some other poor girl across the hall. I don't know what it was about me that attracted her, aside from my clumsiness. Good raw material, maybe.

She invited me to her home for dinner on my next weekend leave, and her father seemed to like me from the start. I was a Scotsman and that was good, and I wasn't a Catholic, which was just as well. I felt accepted. Tommy was determined to keep the family together — a family that now included me because we married.

Tommy would half-cook his breakfast eggs the night before a work morning to save time. He had other odd little ways. He hated flies in a way that suggested an unspoken bad experience with them earlier in his life. Should one dare come into the kitchen, he would smash any cups and plates that got in his way as he leapt about like a madman with his rolled-up paper. Otherwise, he was normal enough and a decent man.

We argued once, when the women were away, about how to cook the saveloys we'd been left for our dinner. He fried and I boiled. Tommy was a small, energetic man. While I stood six foot two, he was five two, but full of vinegar.

When he was young, Tommy had escaped the mines of his village, Newcraighall, southeast of Edinburgh. Nancy, the girl he'd marry, was a lady's maid in the big house on the estate outside the village. They met in the village shop owned by her brother, who'd lost a leg in the mines and turned to shopkeeping. She was helping out behind the counter when Tommy came in to buy his five Woodbines. They sold cigarettes loose in those days.

They married and escaped the village. Nancy's employer helped them get a rented house in the Old Town in Edinburgh. It was the time of the Great Depression.

Tommy was determined that they should own their own home. He went to the council and somehow got a job as a tram driver. They were living in Livingston Place in a two-bedroom house with their two young daughters: tall, dark-haired Mary, and, three years younger, tiny red-haired Rena.

Tommy took his two younger brothers in to live with them, then bought a house in Bellevue and moved his extended family there; all still jammed into a two-bedroom house. One of his brothers, Bobby, had secretly married a woman he'd made pregnant, while continuing to live with Tommy and Nancy and the girls. Tommy flew into one of his rages and threw him out when he discovered the double life.

Nancy, my mother-in-law, searched for the family she'd been separated from as a child. She was born in Glasgow. Her father's name was McGinley. The very mention of him made her shudder. Having given birth to six children, Nancy's mother suffered a stroke and went into hospital where she died.

Her father kept Nancy and sent the other five away to a place called the Black Isle, a peninsula across the bay from Inverness. They were put into the care of farming families who used them as labour. Nancy was sent to a school that trained her as a lady's maid, which she became.

Later, she tracked down her younger sister, Gertrude, who at 14 had married a farm labourer of Irish extraction who had read books and become a socialist and who stirred up his fellow workers on an estate and was sent packing.

Searching for a better life, they'd travelled to New Zealand and settled there. The sisters had exchanged letters through the war years. Gert sent occasional food parcels. After the war, she wrote to Nancy, saying, 'A lot of people from the UK are coming to New Zealand.' That planted a seed.

Tommy was 49 and had been thinking about moving the family to Australia.

I was unhappy. I didn't want to go back to Gattonside. My father had fallen out with one of the local councillors, and when I took Mary down there to live after we'd married we couldn't even rent a house. The councillor had warned everyone off us.

We rented a room in an old lady's place. We went to my parents once a week for a bath. It was humiliating. There was no future. My father wouldn't speak to Mary. He hated the fact that I'd married a townie. He'd had a daughter of a powerful friend lined up for me to marry. I wanted to thrash him.

So, with Mary and her parents and her sister, I put my name down for a passage on an Orient Line ship to New Zealand. The only passages available were first-class. We weren't eligible for an assisted passage. It cost £115 each, which was a lot at the time, but we had no choice.

Mary's younger sister, who was wilful, didn't want to go, didn't want to leave Edinburgh and her pals and all the boys she knew behind, but she didn't have any say.

Mary and I married in Edinburgh. In the photographs everyone is thin. Gaunt, really. Food was still rationed, and whisky almost impossible to find. Almost.

When I told my father of the plan to sail to New Zealand with my new wife's family, he gave me an ultimatum. I had a year to come back. He'd pay my fare to return. Only my fare. If not, I was no longer his son. My mother cried, but didn't protest.

It took a month to sail across the world to New Zealand. Travelling first-class, it was very comfortable, more comfortable than anything I'd ever known. I took up chess, and we lay about in deckchairs and fell in love with the sun.

Mary's sister, who was still in a rage about being dragged away from Edinburgh, used to sneak down to the lower-class decks to flirt with the boys. One afternoon, I walked into her cabin and found her there with one of the officers.

We landed in the capital, Wellington, on a rainy day. We stayed a night in a hotel, the St George in the centre of town, and then took a ferry through wild seas to the South Island and travelled on to Christchurch, where Mary's Uncle George met us at the railway station and we caught a train together, south to a village not much bigger than Gattonside called Hampden, where George and Gert had their chicken farm.

We didn't often have chicken to eat back home in a Scotland already fading in my mind. This place we'd come to was a new thing altogether. The people sounded different, looked different — rougher somehow — smelled different. On that train was the first time I ever saw anyone rolling a cigarette.

But we never looked over our shoulders. This was our home now, and there was no going back. Not ever. Not a thought; certainly not a spoken one.

We'd been married only seven months when we got to Gert and George's place. There were two spare bedrooms — Tommy and I in one, Mary, her mother and little sister in the other. It was a frustrating time. It was a rough place, and George put us to work. He had it all planned: we were to be free labour.

Their son, Georgie, was a surprise. He was about 12, couldn't speak, though he grunted as if he desperately wanted to. The doctors had wanted to send him to Wellington for operations to correct his awful defects, but his father said he wasn't letting him go into a hospital and kept him home as he was.

Later, when they moved down into Dunedin, they always looked for a house people couldn't see into because Georgie frightened people.

We found out about his older sisters later. Gert's first child took fits. She choked and died. Then there were two more girls, Catherine and Veronica. They weren't right either.

Georgie was born next, a mess — double hair-lip and a cleft palate — but at least he was a son, George said, and so Gert took their broken baby boy home. George put the two girls into Seacliff, the big old mental asylum, two train stops south from Hampden towards Dunedin. Gert visited them every week. One of the girls died there in the 1950s, the other in the 1960s. Life in New Zealand was the same as in Scotland, except there was more to eat. And there was no class distinction. As Mary said, all you needed was a little initiative.

We also needed to get out of Hampden. Rena was in a constant state of outrage about the house with its outside toilet and having to share a bed with her big sister, who would rather have been sharing a bed with her new husband, me. Georgie used to come into their room in the mornings, Mary said. Rena would send him running with her screams.

There were other things, too. George Sinclair had, it turned out, had an affair with the girl across the road, and she'd had a baby by him. Things weren't good with us all there, jammed together on that chicken farm with all its secrets. George used to abuse Gert, hit her. Tommy flew into a temper about it one day and confronted him. There was a lot of shouting and arm waving.

Mary and I were there only a few weeks, but it felt a lot longer. A friend of Gert's knew a woman called Olly, who had a big house in Tennyson Street, in the centre of Dunedin, the city to the south. She took an instant liking to us and gave us a room.

The first thing her husband, Gordon, knew about it was when he came home and we were sitting at the dinner table eating. He took it in his stride. He took a lot in his stride with Olly.

When you walked up the stairs at Olly's house, dust would come out of all the borer holes in the wood. Olly's mother had died there, and she was supposed to haunt the place. A proofreader from the local newspaper, *The Otago Daily Times*, rented another room. He was a little bit strange and kept to himself.

There was another room for what Olly called her goodies; stuff she was buying to put in the lovely new house Gordon had promised to build her. She showed us inside that room one day. It was packed to the roof with all sorts of stuff, like expensive china.

She ran up such bills with the big department stores that she was stopping them from being able to afford the new house, though she refused to see it that way. She preferred to think it was all Gordon's fault.

He was a lovely man, a plasterer by trade, and he often plastered in his time off, too. He'd drink down at the old Captain Cook Hotel at the north end of the city. He took me down there the second night after we moved into their house, and got me very drunk and late for dinner.

Gordon ran off with his labourer's wife in the end. They moved south to Mataura, a freezing-works town far south of Dunedin. Her name was Thelma, and she'd been throwing herself at him for months at the pub. The labourer was a bit slow on the uptake and didn't notice until it was too late. Gordon had grown tired of Olly's nagging. He wouldn't fight with her. He'd just walk away, often to the Captain Cook and that labourer's wife.

I went looking for a job. I wanted to be a car mechanic. I'd worked on my father's cars, but I didn't have any qualifications. Being an immigrant seemed to count against me, though there were many Scots living in Dunedin. Failing to land a job fixing cars, I got one as a metal polisher in an engineering factory in the city.

My Scottishness and my work ethic brought a certain amount of resentment from some of the Kiwis. The only immigrants in New Zealand seemed to be either from the UK or Holland. The locals disliked the Dutch the most because they worked so hard. Some of them, it was said, took two jobs.

The company that hired me had just branched into stainless steel, and I specialised in that, becoming a polisher, then a welder and, after a couple of years, foreman.

One day the boss came to me and pointed to a job in the newspaper and said, 'I suppose you'll be applying for this.' I hadn't known about it until he pointed it out. It was for a workshop manager at a company specialising in stainless steel in Invercargill, even further south, right at the bottom of the country.

Mary took it all in her stride. She made friends easily.

Tommy had moved down to Dunedin after us, leaving Nancy in Hampden. He got a job at the Hillside Railway Workshops, a huge clanking place next to the smelly gas works in South Dunedin. Then Nancy and Rena moved down to the city and the family was a family again.

Tommy bought a section on the back of one of the city's many hilly suburbs, Morningside. The quarter-acre he bought was so steep that he had to build three terraces up the backyard to plant a lawn and put in vegetable plots and fruit trees. He paid a deposit and had a brick house built there, looking out across a wide valley of farmland. We all lived there together, with the occasional visitor.

A sailor Rena had been sweet on back in Scotland was so taken with her charms that he followed her all the way to New Zealand. When he turned up at the door, Tommy took pity on him and let him move in for a while.

But Rena didn't fancy him anymore, and she ran off to Wellington where she became a singer with a dance band and even made a couple of records. Then she met another sailor, an English one, and she married him and told the family afterwards — sent them a telegram with the news. Tommy was devastated, though Tommy was quite easily devastated.

Then Mary and I bought a section in Waverley, another hilly Dunedin suburb, though this one was away across the wide harbour from the city.

It seemed everyone in Waverley was our age. We paid £175 for our quarter-acre. We didn't have that much money saved, and when I told the man selling it, he said, 'Just give me 20 and pay the rest off.' He didn't charge us any interest.

Both of our new neighbours had only recently moved into their newly built houses. On one side of us was a sensible brick bungalow with picture windows looking out across the valley to a farm; on the other side a strange flat-roofed concrete house, a cross between a small castle and a toilet block.

We built what we could afford. We both worked down in the city. Mary worked as a typist and secretary in the office of a big department store in the middle of town. Everyone around us was having babies and we thought we should, too. Everyone tried to fit in. People talked if you'd been married two years or more and there were no children.

Our neighbours in the concrete castle were Graham and Nat. Graham, or Gay as they called him, was our old landlady Olly's eldest son, a tall, handsome man with an eye for the ladies, despite being married. Nat became pregnant three times, and lost all the babies at birth or soon after. We went to one of the funerals, but the sight of Gay, in tears carrying that tiny white coffin, was too much for me, and we didn't go to the others. I think they were forced to have funerals then.

Gay believed he was irresistible to women, and this eventually backfired on him. He was arrested and charged with sexual assault after not taking no for an answer at a bottle party.

A bottle party was a Kiwi tradition. It was a party where everyone brought a bottle, or several if it was beer. There'd often be a big punch bowl full of fruit juice and cold tea and fruit, and new arrivals would empty their bottle of spirits into it. People would sometimes get very drunk and behave accordingly.

But there was a great sense of community and of equality, though there were all sorts living around us, like Tom who'd been blinded in the war. He was a lovely man with a big chubby wife and two chubby little daughters. He laid his new lawn in the middle of the night.

By the time we moved to Invercargill, we had two boys, aged eight and five. We bought a house on the eastern boundary of town, near the city cemetery, which the local kids used as a playground.

We were also near the racecourse, and there were stables for racing horses in several of the streets around us. Next to the local grocery store up on the main street was a blacksmith's. The blacksmith himself, a husky, scarred old Scot, lived with his wife in an old wooden house right across the road from us.

He'd taught several of his grandchildren to play the bagpipes, and sometimes, on Sundays, after church, he'd have them marching up and down on his front veranda playing 'Scotland the Brave' or something similar. Terrible din.

There were the usual intrigues in the neighbourhood. Our neighbour on the eastern side had the local butcher's shop. Mick was Irish, and a drunk who beat his wife and terrorised his three daughters.

Back then, being a drunk wasn't out of the ordinary, and, when he was sober, Mick seemed fond of his girls and his wife, though he'd tirelessly lament the lack of a son once he had a few drinks in him. No one ever mentioned that he beat his wife and terrorised his children. It had been the same when I was growing up.

I hadn't wanted children. I really wanted only Mary and for the two of us to have a life together. Of course, my memories of childhood were of the nightmare quality, while hers, as she told them to me, were of a golden time, until the war came along, but she was a teenager by then. And she wanted children, ached for them in fact, so we had children, the two boys, born three years apart in the early 1950s.

The first turned out to be not at all what I expected, though I didn't know what to expect, never having been a son with a proper father. I'd had the sort of father who once moved one of his lady friends into our already crowded house to sleep in the big bed with him while my mother slept with the girls.

He was a pig of a man and a pig of a father, and I was determined not to be a pig of a man. As to being a father, I was unprepared and, at times, jealous of this new little being in Mary's arms. Still, her being so happy made me happy.

Our firstborn grew into a moody and quiet boy, who seemed to keep his own counsel and hardly appeared to need a father at all. He didn't bound and run as I had expected of a son. He hid his head in books, having somehow taught himself to read even before he reached the age of five and started at the local school, and he often unsettled me with his questioning gaze.

He grew tall like me, but never grew useful in any practical sort of way. He announced at an early age that he intended to be an archaeologist when he grew up, and took to studying books about digging up mummies.

He was the absolute apple of his grandfather Tommy's eye, the firstborn of a new generation in a new country, and a boy to boot, though not a boy to kick a ball around with much. Tommy, mad keen on football, hid any disappointment at that and bought him a microscope for his birthday instead.

Our second boy was the opposite of his big brother. He was bouncy and boisterous and full of fun and loud laughter, a happy storm of a kid. It was hard to resist picking him up and throwing him up in the air to catch, just for his shouts of joy.

Our older boy seemed to not much like this new intruder. One day when I was at work and his mother was talking to a neighbour across the hedge, he dragged his baby brother's bassinet out the front door, down the concrete steps, and left it, baby brother and all, at the front gate.

He admitted later, under duress, that he was hoping someone would take his little brother away. I beat him on the bottom with my slipper for that. Mary insisted. I found it hard to do and, at Mary's insistence, I'd have to do it often, though it did little to change my son's character, which was stubborn.

We knew we had to leave the house and the life we'd built in Dunedin to make a better life than we'd have had in Scotland even better. With Mary's eye on the bank balance and my endless hours of overtime, we'd done well, but we could do better, and that job in Invercargill was for a manager, something I'd never dreamed of being, though I knew I could do it.

I was good with men. My time as a sergeant in the Army back in Scotland had given me the confidence to lead others. Perhaps the fact that I knew how to do the work I was asking them to do myself gave me a power another sort of manager mightn't have had. Also, I wouldn't suffer fools or slackers or shoddy work, and most of those who worked with me or for me quickly came to realise that.

Mary made friends easily and quickly and joined us up to the local Presbyterian church, helping with the Sunday School classes and dragging me along on Sundays with our boys, cheeks and knees shining, hair parted as straight as rulers.

I'd never been inside a church before I met Mary, and never felt easy in the places with their awful songs and worse ministers, but I felt proud standing next to her with our boys, though the eldest generally looked unhappy about being there.

I didn't find being a father quite as easy as Mary found being a mother. I made it clear to the boys at various times that if they had any questions about anything, girls and that sort of thing, they should just ask me, though they never did. But mainly I concentrated on making as much money as I could and getting in a decent vegetable garden, which turned out to be the measure of a man in New Zealand.

I never missed my old life in Scotland, not for a moment, and my father was as good as his word. After a year, he had my mother write to me saying I'd hear no more from him and he would not be expecting to see me anytime soon, if ever again. Those are the words she wrote: 'If ever again'.

It hurt me to read them, but I had no regrets, except the distance from my sisters, especially Cathy, the closest to me in age and the one of the five I loved the most, though I loved them all.

She and Mary wrote to each other regularly, so I was kept in touch with things back there, though thankfully little about the man who was my father.

My mother would write, behind his back she said, but her letters were short and didn't say much about anything except the weather and a little of my sisters' news. Mary would write back. She seemed to keep in touch with everyone she'd ever known, along with almost everyone she was related to.

I hardly ever wrote at all, not being confident about my choice of words or my spelling, having been pulled from school so early, and there never having been much in the way of books in our house when I was young. I left that to Mary, who also taught me to dance, though never to have the confidence to stand up before a roomful of people and speak. There were always other men around who liked doing that sort of thing and I let them get on with it.

My general manager in Invercargill was a foot shorter than me, and always seemed to try to make up for it in my presence by talking a great deal in a loud, knowing way. He reminded me, in that, of my father, though I didn't let him get under my skin. We were a good combination, and the company became so successful that it expanded north to Christchurch, taking us with it, though not all of us. The stubborn son stayed. He was 17 by then and keen to leave home, I think. I understood that, but his mother found it hard.

He had started in a job where he worked nights and, without his presence, a calm had fallen upon our evenings at home. I felt I might like him more from a distance, and that turned out to be true.

# TUESDAY

It's a grey, cold Invercargill day, but, wonderfully, there's no wind. Gordie and I meet in the hotel foyer and take ourselves out of the Kelvin's glass doors at 8am, hang a right and stroll around the corner to the only local café I know of coffee repute, Zookeepers, a block to the south, on Tay Street.

Tay is as heroically wide as Invercargill's other great central boulevard, Dee, which, like Tay, Esk, Don and several Invercargill streets, is named after a Scottish river, och aye and hoots bloody mon.

And if that sounds a tad sarky, then maybe it is, because, although I'm absolutely pulsing with Scottish blood, I grew up in a family that was slightly ambivalent about the whole Scottish thing. Well, with the exception of my grandfather, who was known to put on a kilt and do a bit of the hippety-hoppety dancing without much encouragement, but that was about as far as things went with us, and some of us thought Grandad and the dancing was a bit embarrassing, looked the other way and certainly didn't join in.

There was no affection for the skirl of the pipes; no one joined any of the many Scottish clubs that proliferated in places like Dunedin and Invercargill. Mum listened to Mario Lanza, not Jimmy Shand. Dad was fond of Dean Martin.

Dee and Tay streets meet a big block down from the Zookeepers Café, at the Boer War Memorial, which has long stood as a towering and strange centrepiece to

Invercargill's most popular traffic roundabout. On each of the four corners of this great Invercargill intersection, there used to be a bank building, which is why they call it Bank Corner. Three remain. It was always the windiest spot in town, and groovy girls in mini-skirts in the late 1960s had to look out for their dignity turning that corner.

People don't mention it much now, but Invercargill was once a good-looking place apparently. It still has the bones of what it was in the late 1800s, when it was a growing town with a surprisingly handsome combination of streets and buildings. 'Where once there were unsightly swamps,' *The Southland Times* wrote excitedly in 1878, 'there are now blocks of elegant buildings.'

The transformation of the muddy and makepiece frontier town into a place of architectural charm was mainly due to the work of a Scotsman called FW Burwell, who moved to Invercargill in the early 1870s and set about creating a town centre of comely Renaissance-style two- and three-storey buildings.

The depression of the 1880s put an end to all the building, and sadly a lot of Burwell's work was later destroyed or remodelled, but for a while back there Invercargill was, so they said, quite a sight to see.

The sight confronting me at the moment is Gordie tucking into a great steaming plate of mince on toast. 'Bloody good,' he announces. It's that rich dark brown colour that bloody good mince should be, but it's all a bit early for me and almost more than I can bear, even looking at it, not to mention getting big meaty steamy whiffs of it across the table.

I order toast and jam. The coffee is very good here, and nearly as strong as the stuff in Kingston. The last time I visited this place, which, in a bid to live up to its name, is full of unsettling Dada-meets-Disney statuary, the owner, an understated bloke with loud thoughts, wrote a message in the creamy top of my flat white each morning I visited. The first morning it said 'stranger', as if to remind me I was from another place, which was a bit out of line, I thought.

I'd spent my formative years in Invercargill, after all. I was living here in this little-known city at the end of the world from the innocent age of eight until I was a less-innocent 21, when I escaped, as we used to say in those days.

Gordie escaped, too, but his escape was a bit more complicated. He made the mistake, at one point, of going back. The paper enticed him to return for an outrageous grade rise. But it didn't work out. 'You can't go back' is all he'll say about it now.

Invercargill is really quite easy to like, right up until you leave the place and start seeing it through new eyes from the outside. Though, of course, Invercargill was really never even meant to be here in the first place.

Way back in 1844, a surveyor called Frederick Tuckett was commissioned and sent down to the bottom of the South Island to find a suitable site for a new Scottish Presbyterian settlement. Fred, who was a Quaker from Bristol, had worked with the legendary engineer Brunel on the Great Western Railway in England.

He looked all over the southern coast for a likely spot, and he wasn't in the least impressed by the bit of land where Invercargill is now, if you could even call it land at the time. He supposedly said it was a bog 'unfit for human habitation', and went back north a bit and settled instead on the spot where Dunedin, or 'New Edinburgh', is now.

But there's another version of that story which claims the whalers and sealers, who had settled along the Southland coast, married local Maori women and raised families, weren't keen on too much settlement coming to the area, and the rules and the changes that a local population boom might bring.

They'd been there quite a while and developed their own rules. So they made a point of guiding the surveyor to the worst possible parts of the south, including the swamps and dense unfriendly forest where Invercargill sits now, which kept everyone away for a while longer.

The first white man who saw any hope in Invercargill was an Irishman called John Kelly, who built a rough house at the mouth of the Otepuni Stream, which now runs in a decorative manner through the city's centre. Kelly, a religious type, lived there with his wife and what the history books describe as his 'assorted children'.

Then he built a wharf to encourage shipping, and, once he was settled in, he tried to buy the adjacent 40-acre site from the Government, but, noting that there was interest in it, the politicians kept the land for themselves, had the place surveyed for a settlement, chopped down the forest, drained the land, and planted the seeds of the city of Invercargill.

The shallow estuary served as the region's port until Bluff, just south with its deep and capacious harbour, stole most of the shipping away by the late 1880s, though the

Invercargill port was kept ticking over with a bit of low-end coastal shipping until it finally closed in the early 1960s.

It was from there that the crazy wooden the railway to Winton had set out. The remains of the wharf and the railway are still there, a bit forlorn and overlooked, down below the bridge that runs across the river mouth to Invercargill Airport and on to the end of the road at Oreti Beach. Next to the old wharf, there's a small steam engine sitting on some wooden rails. It's a full-sized replica of the original loco, the *Lady Barkly*, and I suspect hardly anyone visits her much anymore.

Growing up in Invercargill, I never knew much of the city's history. No one ever said anything about it, and it was hardly a compulsory subject at school. When we moved there at the end of the 1950s, Mum and Dad settled

us into a new house they had bought in one of the new suburbs of the era. Hawthorndale was out on the city's eastern fringes abutting the sprawling Eastern Cemetery and a short bike ride from the Otepuni Creek, which was a natural playground for the kids of the area.

I'd lived on the outskirts of the city in Dunedin, too, right on the edge where the country started, which is almost as good a gift as living on the edge of the ocean. I spent all my spare time after school in Invercargill off in the bush with my pals, launching rafts in the creek, building forts and fomenting wild schemes.

Once we managed, for a brief period, to dam the Puni, as we called the creek, so effectively that the council had to send men in overalls out to undo our mischief, as we watched wide-eyed from the undergrowth. There may even have been a story in *The Southland Times* about it.

Today, Gordie and I are heading out west to Riverton and, hopefully, far beyond. Far, far beyond, if I have my way. Gordie's keen to see Riverton. It's where he was born, in December of 1950, in the district hospital that used to sit at the entrance to town out there. It was later turned from a general hospital into a geriatric hospital, and then closed altogether.

My first mother-in-law, who had the lovely name Ora, was a patient there, not because she was geriatric, but because she had multiple sclerosis. In those days, because there were no separate facilities for sufferers of that awful degenerative disease, they were put in with the oldies, many of whom were suffering dementia. It wasn't a happy place to visit, as I recall.

Out at the far northern edge of Invercargill, we turn left for Riverton at the big roundabout, past the old White House pub, once famous for having the longest bar in the southern hemisphere, now mainly famous only for surviving at all in these anti-drinking, move-to-the-city times. It used to be a freezing-workers' pub and was best avoided back then.

When I was growing up, Invercargill was a freezing-works town, surrounded by the huge meat factories. At their peak, before they started closing or downsizing, those killing factories were slaughtering 7 million animals a year, mostly sheep.

It's a wonder we couldn't smell the blood in the wind, though maybe we could and we just didn't know it. Southland was proud of its meat-making reputation. When I was at primary school, as part of our wider cultural education, my class was taken for a visit to the Alliance Freezing Works, across the road from the White House.

Little girls screamed, and one even fainted at the sight of the great queue of sheep having their throats cut by blood-spattered men with fast knives. I threw up in the stomach-wrenching stench of the tannery section. The class bully turned white.

The ambition of many Southland schoolboys back then was to end up with a job on the killing chain out at the freezing works. It wasn't my dream job, and nor was it Gordie's. We both had our sights set on slightly higher things, at much lower pay.

The freezing works, especially if you could get a job on that killing chain, paid extremely well, everyone used to say.

It was local legend. And it was seasonal, so you'd get a few months off at a time to do something else, or nothing at all. But, even if I hadn't wanted to be a newspaper reporter, that school trip to the works would have put me off any such ambition. I couldn't even look at a sausage for days after that.

Being on this particular piece of road right now with Gordie gets me thinking out loud about a pub crawl we'd gone on with a crowd from *The Southland Times*. It was probably 1969, and I don't recall whether it was an office-sanctioned affair, but we were all in a bus rolling about the Southland Plains from country pub to country pub, getting drunker and crazier all the way, as we did on Saturday nights in those days.

And it would have been a Saturday, because that was the only night of the morning-newspaper week that we all generally had off. 'Something bad happened on that pub crawl,' I tell Gordie. 'Not really bad, like sheep buggery or murder, but something I've always felt bad about.' I'm not sure why I'm telling him this.

For some reason back then, perhaps because of turning 18, I'd been given my grandfather's old pocket-watch, a heavy silver thing with engraving inside the lid, with his name and some other details I also now, to my shame, don't recall.

What I do, to my shame, recall is that I was in the habit at the time of carrying that pocket-watch in my own pocket, and I lost it that night, after staggering out of the last pub on that pub crawl and falling into a drainage ditch across the road.

I might have been in there a while. I might have slept or thrown up, possibly a bit of both. Luckily it must have been a dry drainage ditch at the time, because I didn't drown. Luckily also, the bus driver must have been keeping a head count, because I was eventually retrieved by my workmates, only to wake up the next day, hungover in Invercargill, minus my grandad's watch.

'I haven't ever told anyone about it 'til now,' I tell Gordon. 'I'm still a bit afraid Mum might ask about that watch one day and I won't be able to lie. I also wonder,' I babbled on, 'whether that watch is still lying out there in that drainage ditch.'

Gordie shoots me a meaningful glance. 'I've got a feeling that pub was out this way,' he says, turning off Highway 99 just after Wrights Bush at a sign for a place called Thornbury, which turns out to be home to a virtual village of farm-machinery museums, all of them closed. There's a pub, too, and it fits the misty map of our memory of that country pub on that long-ago night.

'Do you remember the reporter who got so drunk he climbed a tree and had a wank?' asks Gordie.

'Good God.'

I don't recall that, thankfully. I might have been in the drainage ditch at the time. We park and I wander off looking for the drainage ditch, but it's not there across the road from the pub or anywhere nearby.

'I suppose it was a while ago,' I say to Gordie. Forty-five years, when we think about it, but that pub looks right. It's two storeys tall and stark against the sky. No tree, though.

It seems like there's no one about in Thornbury, but then we spot a driver sitting quietly in the cab of his truck, parked outside one of the farm-machinery museums. Gordie wanders over and engages him without delay. The truck's a big covered-in one, giving its contents away when they suddenly take umbrage at their confinement and make the truck shake and rattle with their angry cattle kicks and butts.

'They'll get over it,' says the driver, a rugged individual, but friendly and seemingly open to Gordie's sudden conversation.

'We're on a road trip,' he tells the man with the truckful of cattle. 'We think we were at this pub a few years back. It would have been 1969 probably. Was there ever a tree outside it?'

'I wasn't born until 1976,' says the driver, which pretty much closes the conversation down. Anyway, he needs to get those poor beasts in the back of his truck off to wherever they're bound, a slaughterhouse probably. It's still a bit early for us to have a drink at the Thornbury pub, I suppose. It doesn't look open anyway. Actually, Thornbury itself doesn't seem open.

In the olden days things were much worse for many of the drinkers of Southland. In a terrible turn of events, the whole of Invercargill wasn't open for a drink for nearly 40 years after the citizens voted in a total prohibition of liquor sales in 1905.

Quite what drove them to this extreme may have been down to a fatal combination of God-bothering and bad behaviour. Living down here in the early days, up to your armpits in mud and freezing your ears off, can't have been easy, and alcohol would have been some solace and was doubtless embraced. And, being mainly of Scottish and Irish stock, those old settler types came with drunken genes anyway.

As a result, there was an enthusiastic temperance movement across the province. Mataura voted itself dry in 1902, and Invercargill followed the terrible trend three years later, but only by a margin of nine votes.

Prohibition backfired, as that sort of thing does, and drinking enthusiastically and illegally continued thanks to a steady supply of booze brought in from pubs and various merchants in adjoining country districts, outside the alcohol-free zone enforced around the city.

Enormous volumes of beer in kegs were smuggled to private homes in the town, and sold by the glass by the men they were calling 'keggers' in hidden portable drinking spots dotted around Invercargill.

Then, when prohibition was finally voted out in the mid-1940s by thirsty troops coming home from the war, a committee of local do-gooders persuaded the Government to grant a monopoly on all liquor sales to a newly created Invercargill Licensing Trust.

The bloke who championed the move was the local Labour MP of the time, William Mortimer Clarence Denham, or WMC as he liked to be known. Oddly, and perhaps in redemption, Denham also fought for a special Government fund to help New Zealand writers have their work published, creating what would become the Literary Grants Advisory Board.

But bugger him anyway for limiting the drinking options in Invercargill, where a local brewery still has trouble finding taps on Trust-controlled bars, and for fuelling the boozehound culture of the south.

The idea for a licensing trust was borrowed from an English scheme that returned all profits from liquor sales to city amenities. As a result, to this day alcohol is dispensed to the drinkers of Invercargill a little like Pharmac distributes those other drugs to the general populace. You can't, for instance, buy beer or wine at the local supermarkets.

Perhaps as a result of all of these attempts to control it, drinking was a big part of the culture in the south when Gordie and I were growing up, though mainly it seemed it was more of a male thing. Women drank, but it was generally the men who drank too much.

When I was a kid, I'd regularly hear our next-door neighbour in Hawthorndale, through the hedge between our houses, spewing his beer-filled insides out on his lawn late of an evening. It was part of the night-time soundscape in our street.

The neighbour's name was Mick and he ran the local butcher's shop. People in the neighbourhood spoke well of his sausages. He'd sometimes pop over to our place bearing a couple of flagons of beer in a vain bid to get Dad to drink more than he'd planned. But Mick would generally suck up that beer all by himself, as if he was desperate to get to the bottom of every bottle he got his hands on. One evening he knocked himself out walking into a glass door we had in our hall.

My dad never seemed to drink too much. Well, not that it showed. And he didn't go to the pub after work with the other men from work, though that may have been part of the loneliness of him being the manager at his factory, where they made stainless-steel tanks for the many dairy factories of Southland, and stainless-steel urinals for the many pubs. I think the theory was that he couldn't mix socially with the men he was in charge of for fear they'd take advantage of the situation.

So it was Dad's habit to come straight home from work each evening, open the flagon of beer he'd left in the fridge, and quietly drink it as he read the paper or listened to the wireless and smoked a few Pall Malls while Mum put the finishing touches to tea. I don't recall him ever being drunk or even affected by the beer, though he must have regularly demolished half a gallon of it.

With his unaffected ways, Dad probably got me thinking that drinking was a good and manly thing to do. I don't know, but I do know I've been a drinker all my life, and that it hasn't always been such a good thing to be.

And I've seen what it has done to others around me, but I never really, as a kid anyway, had the faintest inkling that there was anything bad about booze. It was alluring. It was one of the three things you were allowed to do when you were grown-up, along with smoking cigarettes and having sex. I suppose we were already smoking.

I had a school friend whose mother had a rich old daddy who owned an eel factory out Mossburn way. Her husband, my friend's father, wasn't around anymore. She was a divorcée, which was quite a scandalous thing to be in Southland in those days. Less scandalous, she was also an alcoholic.

When I stayed at my pal's place sometimes, I did notice that his mother, who was always nice enough to me, would drink beer at breakfast time and quietly segue to sherry and maybe something even stronger later on. She'd go to bed early, leaving us to explore her liquor supplies, drink some of the gimlet and the Merry Widow from their bottles in the cocktail cabinet, and water them down to get the levels up so that she wouldn't notice, as if.

One night we were playing The Rolling Stones too loud on the stereogram after she'd gone to bed, and she came into the room screaming, waving a big pair of scissors and trying to cut the power lead to stop the music. We had to wrestle her to the floor to save her from frying herself, not to mention ruining the stereo.

My friend's big brother would buy beer for us, though he'd charge us a service fee. If we had the money for a dozen bottles, he'd keep three bottles for himself. He was two or three years older than us and looked ready to thump us if we tried to renegotiate the deal.

We didn't complain, but we worked hard for our beer money. We'd pick potatoes in farmers' fresh-turned fields, and gather pinecones and sell them door-to-door around town to raise money for beer. We were aged around 13 or 14 at the time.

I had another friend at high school whose father had built a still in their backyard and made his own whisky out there, in the old moonshine way. It was illegal then, and it was raw and rough stuff and too much for our young and sensitive palates, though we did give it a few tries.

At high school, we'd sometimes slip away if we had a free period together, take off any identifying parts of our uniforms, go in and buy booze ourselves from the bottle store down the road, and bike down to Thomson's Bush to drink it. Then sometimes we'd even wobble back to school for biology or algebra at the end of the day. No wonder I didn't pass the UE exams.

I don't recall the first time I was ever drunk, but, whenever it was or in whatever circumstances, the experience did nothing to stop me doing the same thing again and again, even to this day occasionally, though I comfort myself by saying to myself that I'm not in such a bad way with that sort of thing as some of my friends.

After work many nights at *The Southland Times*, some of us — reporters, subs, a few printers, though never any of the readers — would settle down for an hour or two or three playing poker for money and drinking, beer usually. No one drank wine in those days.

Then Spud and I would wander back to the flat in Ythan Street under the glow of the rising sun, stop at Lange's, the big bakery on the way, and pick up fresh-made pies. Then we'd pull the curtains and sleep until noon or later, eat something and head back to work for a four or a six o'clock start. I preferred a six o'clock start with the two o'clock finish. It felt like I was in another world.

And all the while that we were learning our trade in the middle of the night, we were hearing a soundtrack of tall tales from our elders concerning the many wild journalists who'd gone before us at the *Times*, the ones who'd gone off to sparkling careers or early death.

The stories almost always involved drunkenness and bad, sometimes insane behaviour, which, when fused together, seemed to form a badge of honour, something young chaps like Spud and myself were taking in, open-eared and wide-eyed, so keen to lose any innocence we had left.

Years later, in the late 1970s, when I'd slipped from the serious grip of *The New Zealand Herald* and joined the wild and doomed *Auckland Star*, a boozy old face from my past popped up, Garth George, though not the one I'd known, not the one who'd said 'Fuck off, Hogg.'

That Garth might have had a twinkle in his eye. This new one was a twinkle-free zone, back from his self-made Hell, having fallen to the gutter, as he put it, when his unquenchable drinking finally spun him out of control, making him difficult to employ. I seem to recall hearing he lost the last bit of his personal plot when he was on-air doing the news for a radio station in Rotorua or somewhere similar.

Then, having hit the bottom, Garth had risen again through the intervention of the Lord, and the Salvation Army, something the born-again Garth would mention regularly. Now the rest of us were the ones who had to be pried from pubs, while he stayed back at the office smoking cigarettes, sipping coffee and eyeing the cute cadets. 'I'd rather be up her than up country' was one of his favourite phrases. Another that I recall went, 'She didn't get lips like that smoking cigarettes.'

It was only after Garth died in 2015 and I read his obituary that I realised he'd already served 10 long years at *The Southland Times* before Gordie and I bounced through the door. Poor bugger.

We started work early at *The Auckland Star*, and we'd generally be out and off to our regular pub by three o'clock, half-crazed from the intensity of making a newspaper and really quite keen for a drink. There was a hard core to our drinking crew and, to make things simple for the bar staff, we all drank the same thing, vodka and tonic, with as much as possible of the former and a mere hint of the latter.

We drank by the round, so it was an organised sort of drunkenness, with an edge of competitiveness, but drinking has always been a competitive sport in New Zealand. Then we'd drive home, half-cut and late for dinner, to our families, or what remained of them. At work on Saturday mornings, when we'd all be feeling rough from Friday nights, we'd send over to the nearby watersiders' pub, which opened early, for breakfast-time vodkas we called heart-starters.

I think it seemed heroic, or something similar, at the time. I don't think we knew how crazy we were. It took someone from the outside to notice that sort of detail.

Sometime during that period, my parents came to Auckland to stay with me, and I thought it might be a good idea to take them along to a birthday dinner we were having for one of my newspaper workmates at a nice Chinese restaurant in Herne Bay.

I must have thought it would be a relaxed and natural opportunity for Mum and Dad to meet some of the people

I worked with at the *Star* and get a little insight into my world. I'd bought the birthday boy a beautiful cut-crystal wine goblet, all wrapped up nicely, looking just like what it was — a bloody expensive wine glass.

I had second thoughts about the plan when we arrived at the restaurant to find my table of revellers in full roar, and the birthday boy, an older guy, absolutely off his face. In fact so off his face that when I handed him my gift, he seized it with a wild-eyed yell of delight and promptly bit a great chunk out of it.

I glanced across at my mother at this point, to observe actual terror on her dear old face. Dad looked like he wanted to hit someone but couldn't decide which one of us, so they went home early, leaving me with my awful friends. Nothing was said about it over breakfast the next day, or indeed ever.


It has turned into a sweet, warm day by the time we roll over the hill where the hospital Gordie was born in used to be, and down into Riverton, which is perhaps Southland's most pleasant place to dream of living in, if a person was to be quite mad enough to ever dream of living again in Southland.

Riverton, an old settlement in terms of non-Maori New Zealand, is a town in two parts. The first bit, the oldest part of town, sits on the flat at the river mouth, and the second, Riverton Rocks as it's called, is across the narrow bridge, hard left, past the fishing lighter basin and up over a steep rise and down again to a grand, south-facing beach.

The old Soundshell's still there, sitting above the sandy beach at the Rocks, but there's a slight bedragglement about the place they used to call, without irony, the Riviera of the South. We drift on along the narrow road above the rocky shore, past houses, cribs, a café, all ranged up the sunny brow of the rising land on our right, resolutely facing the view south and the winds that come all the way, without anything to stop them, from Antarctica. There's Stewart Island out there, seeming closer than it really is.

Looking back across the bay beyond Riverton's river mouth, the line of land is so low that it's barely discernible above the sea. We are — and it doesn't half feel like it — at the edge. But there are advantages to that, like the mussels and paua down there, just below on the rocks for the taking, if you know where to look and you take only what you can eat and no more.

The old Riverton Bowling Club's for sale, as it was the last time I was here, along with quite a number of houses, sitting hopeful behind their real estate signs in the sun. We stop for a coffee at the café, the Beach House, where Gordie immediately sets about interrogating the one customer, luckily a local.

'Is the skating rink still here?' he wants to know, recalling skating there next to the Soundshell when he was a kid to 'I Want To Be Bobby's Girl', a perky pop song of the time.

To better set the scene, Gordie belts out a bit of the song. If the local's alarmed, he doesn't show it. He lights another fag and gazes out at all that sea like he's not really seeing it. I, on the other hand, find the outlook hypnotising and hard to wrench my eyes away from.

Down at the Soundshell, the glamour has definitely departed, and the skating rink is long disappeared and built over. A small group of hard-faced men in matching overalls are chipping unenthusiastically at the weeds in the cracks in the concrete, Community Service workers by their demeanour. The Riverton Soundshell, sitting pointing out at the sea, is smaller than I recall, and made a touch grimmer by the big wire fuck-off fence that's been slung up rudely across the front of the stage.

A memory comes back of being up there on the stage with half the crowd and some band at a long-ago New Year's Eve concert. I think we were all singing 'Feliz Navidad', a popular hit of the time.

Gordon used to come here at Christmases with his family when he was a kid, staying at one of the holiday cottages at Riverton Rocks owned by the Women's Division of Federated Farmers, which his mum was a member of, as all good farmers' wives were then. It must have seemed like some sandy sort of heaven to a farm kid from land-locked Wyndham. He smiles just talking about it. I hope he's not going to sing 'I Want To Be Bobby's Girl' again.

Riverton, as a town starting out, dates back to the 1820s, though there were white men here quite a lot earlier, when first sealers and then whalers started coming ashore to stay around Foveaux Strait and its islands, taking up with local women, marrying, making babies, intermingling and building a new little society.

In the very early days, the Pakeha sealers would seek hospitality at the various Maori villages, some on Rakiura (Stewart Island), others on nearby islands and on the southern coast of the mainland. But they'd sometimes overstay their welcome with their rough and horny ways, and so the Ngai Tahu chiefs of the region decided to create a separate settlement for them and their Maori wives on Codfish Island, which was close enough but far away enough, too.

It might have been as early as 1805 when this carefully considered mixed-race settlement was created. It prospered and, as the sealers built wooden huts and turned instead to fishing and farming and coastal trading, this newly created race bred and spread to the mainland, eventually outnumbering full-blooded Maori in the region. By the 1880s, more than half the population of Southland was of mixed race or, as they said in those days, 'half-caste'.

It wasn't a totally seamless integration, of course. Even after Pakeha were established in the area, the local

Maori had a fierce reputation and there were some fatal misunderstandings. A tourist, a German who enjoyed playing the violin, was discovered by a band of local warriors, attracted by the plaintive sound of his instrument, which he'd made the mistake of playing on a beach in the locality.

The hapless German was seized, carried off, then slaughtered, cooked and eaten. Legend has it the feasters were so enthusiastic that they even ate his violin strings. And, no, they don't say that sometimes on still nights you can hear the dead German's ghostly violin-playing.

Around the same dangerous sort of time, a local chief, dubbed Old Jacob by the whalers, had such a remarkable moko on his face that he had to flee the area and go into hiding for fear he'd lose his life to the then-booming trade in preserved heads. It was Old Jacob whose name was taken, at first, for the new settlement, which became known as Jacob's River, though the Maori called it Aparima, for its river.

By the mid-1800s, the seals had been slaughtered almost out of existence, whaling was in decline, and farming and sawmilling were the town's new reasons for being. There was a busy port here, too, but the erection of a badly judged jetty altered the sea's currents, changed the harbour's contours, and ruined it for commerce.

Now, as it has been for the past 100 years, Riverton home to only a handful of fishing boats and. Of course, it has long been Southland's favourite seaside resort town, though it looks as if that doesn't quite mean what it used to.

\*

Back on Highway 99, we head west, around and over the headland and down to Colac Bay, a big, beautiful sandy smile of a bay, the land again so low rolling back from the sea that there are two roads running in parallel across it. The low one is right on the edge of the beach, lined by an ugly wall of boulders, bulldozed there to stop the waves taking the road, as they do sometimes under the influence of full moons and storms.

And they sometimes get substantial storms in these parts. There's odd evidence here and there. Very odd evidence. We find one strange piece as we investigate what might lurk out of sight up Colac Bay's small offering of side streets.

We get a flash of something large and yellow lurking through the shrubbery down one of them. At first glance, it's the largest lemon in the world, a Meyer with a cockpit and tiny windows, like eyes.

But it's not a large lemon; it's a craft, mounted on a low stage of decking on its own little bit of grassed reserve, looking like a cross between a boat and the cockpit bit of an airliner. It's a sort of survival capsule, we decide. There's no plinth or anything to explain it or how it got here, or the other big question, which is: Why? And there's no one anywhere to ask. I'm not sure we even saw a single car on the ride here from Riverton.

On closer examination, the odd craft, with the words *Anangel Happiness Piraeus* and *Captain Phillips Survival* stencilled on its side, is some sort of life craft, the sort that might be jettisoned with a small selection of survivors from some stricken ship, that ship being, I suppose, the *Anangel*

*Happiness* out of the Greek port of Piraeus. Inside it are some mean-looking little metal bunks. There are dials and gauges, and everything is sealed steel, an indestructible unit that would probably refuse to sink no matter how wild the seas.

Gordie, the unstoppable newshound, is determined to know the story behind the great lemon lifeboat, and so he takes us driving along the Colac Bay beachfront and parks outside the Pavilion, the local café.

I can hear him inside shouting questions at whoever's behind the counter. Maddeningly for Gordie, the shop assistant doesn't know anything about it. 'Well, that's what they say,' I tell him, which isn't particularly helpful as the investigation's not over. Down the road, Gordie pulls over and stops a big sweaty jogger who has lumbered up from the beach and onto the road. Gordie jumps out and waves him down.

The man doesn't look very happy about being stopped, mid-jog, but Gordie will not be denied. 'What's the story with that big yellow lifeboat thing down the beach?' he asks, getting straight to the point and with something of the style of a country copper.

Knowing that there's no escape, the unhappy jogger gets his breath back and admits he knows all about it. The odd craft was found after a storm, floating empty, out to sea from Colac Bay. Some enterprising local went out, towed it in, dragged it up and turned it into accommodation for surfers.

The mystery solved, we can happily leave Colac Bay, on the way out spotting a saggy, peeling old wooden house with a smiley mouth painted beneath its big-eye windows. On the side, in fading paint, it declares *Still Happily Married*.

We're on lonely Highway 99 again, heading out beyond Colac Bay and past Round Hill. They often name things for what they just plain are in these parts, though there are the mysteries we don't get around to investigating.

For instance, back there out beyond Thornbury, there's a place called Gropers Bush, which is a little too far inland to be a reference to the local sea fish and, so, faintly disturbing.

Gordie is singing along to the CD in the car. It's his CD, so he knows most of the words. It's a CD version of a mix tape, and there's a lot of modern stuff on it by people I've never heard of. I've brought the new ZZ Top album to play, but I'm not sure now.

We turn off to Cosy Nook, a tiny clutch of old banged-together cribs at the edge of a saw-toothed rocky bay where there's a boat ramp. By its appearance, it might be somewhere in the Hebrides, except it's Southland and today it's sunny.

The artist Nigel Brown lives back up the road, his personal patch made strikingly obvious by the eye-catching panel of protest he's erected at the roadside, lamenting, in his amazing cinemascopic art and his distinctive script, the neglect of the coast by the local authorities.

There's a lot of detail, and he does seem rather *pissed off*. The trees all lean at 45 degrees away from the southerlies. Nigel's a brave artist.

Nearby Monkey Island is named, history has it, for its resemblance to the head of an ape, but it doesn't look remotely like a chimp or even an orangutan from any angle. It's hardly even what you'd think of as an island, being little

more than a large and lumpy rock connected to the beach at low tide by a short natural causeway.

On we roll along this melancholy coast to Orepuki, a town that has moved three times, with apparently near-fatal results. Originally, it was sited near Monkey Island, which is a short distance south. The town grew from the miners who settled there while they sluiced fine gold from the sand of the beach.

Running out of space quite early on, they moved the town, buildings and all, a few miles to Garfield, where the enthusiastic miners ended up sluicing right into the town, necessitating its final move to its present site, where its population peaked at 3000 citizens, though that was quite some time ago.

There's not much left of Orepuki these days, and there hasn't been for quite some time by the look of things.

Way back in 1960, when the town's new post office was opened, the local paper wrote the place off as a ghost town, enraging the few locals left then.

There's still an ugly pub and a few houses, but not much else. The largest building in Orepuki's main street is an ancient drapery, Adamson & Son Outfitters, long-abandoned and sheathed in big, rusty iron panes as if it holds some secret that must be sealed in.

Back down on the nearby coast at a place called Gemstone Beach, we stumble on a miner, sluicing the sand for gold the old way, using the stream at the eastern end of the beach, showing us the glitter as the sand is washed off and the traces of gold are revealed. He reckons he makes about $300 every couple of weeks, which might go quite a long way in Orepuki.

His name is Rod, 'but they call me Dump Rat,' he says. Take away his wrap-around sunglasses and he might

be an olden-day goldminer with his mighty beard and his leathery, out-in-the-weathery look.

Gordie gets him yakking away. In a brief pause in the talk, I ask Dump Rat about Orepuki. 'What's the talk in town?' I want to know.

There's been a big falling-out, he says, between two of the town's leading figures. 'They had an argument,' says the Rat, 'a stabbing kind of an argument.'

We'd stay for more of this but, just down the road, Tuatapere's calling, though when we get there I become confused and choose the wrong café for lunch. I forgot that there was another one a bit further down the main drag of this charismatic old timber town, which probably does more tourism than timber these days. We have whitebait omelettes, but there's hardly any whitebait in them and they'd be awful omelettes anyway.

Tuatapere tried to brand itself some years back as the Sausage Capital of New Zealand after a local sausage-maker won an award. The sign's still up and there's a butcher still open for business, but it's a slightly embarrassing claim to fame and the faded cartoon sausage on the Tuatapere sign at the edge of town seems to suggest the locals might think so, too.

They'd be better off boasting about trees and how they chopped down and sawed up pretty much all of the beech and broadleaf forests that once grew right through here, stretching down from Fiordland and out across the plains. There's a lovely little slice of what's left of the bush and forest still standing next to the Tuatapere Domain. And there are bits and pieces of bush at various points, scattered across Southland, but mere hints of what must have been.

Before the disruptive white settlers came, Southland's plains were endless bush and forest, interrupted only by rivers, tussock and the swamp of the coastal areas. Shamelessly, the settlers often named their areas of settlement after the bush they'd cleared away for their farms.

There are around 20 so-called 'bushes' across the province, many of them not towns so much as districts. There's Centre Bush, Eastern Bush, Mabel Bush, Roslyn Bush, Seaward Bush, Gummies Bush, Wrey's Bush, Wrights Bush and Grove Bush.

Gummies Bush, just north of Riverton, was named after a local pig farmer, James Leader, who was known to his friends as Gummie, for — you guessed it — having no teeth. Grove Bush, southwest of Invercargill, has a slightly more inspiring claim to fame, though hardly anyone remembers now.

It was the birthplace of Frank Forde, an amazing athlete around the turn of the twentieth century and a world-beater at the hammer throw. Frank was one of nine kids, and his father and brothers were all outstanding athletes of various persuasions. In fact his older brother William was known as Medally Bill for the number of competitions he'd won.

It was Frank, though, who grabbed the spotlight after he attended the Irish Athletic Society's annual sports day in Invercargill in 1905 and threw the 7-kilo hammer a good metre and a half beyond the then-current world record.

When his new record was disallowed after a discrepancy over the weight of the hammer, he promptly challenged the record again and, watched by a large crowd of excited locals a few days later, he officially exceeded even his previous throw by a good distance.

Then, the following year, Frank caused a sensation up in Dunedin when, at the Caledonian Sports, he set another world record, throwing a 10-kilo hammer 31.4 metres. He went on to rack up major successes over the years in the long jump, wrestling, caber tossing and other strenuous events. They called him 'New Zealand's invincible all-round athlete'.

Gordie is increasingly distracted by his tweets, which are picking up a following, small but growing by the day. By the hour, he reckons. He posted a picture of the bowling club for sale in Riverton, and it's more popular than the cheese rolls at Kingston. He might help finally sell the Riverton Bowling Club. It does have a great view. There's a lot of lawn to cut, though.

Beyond Tuatapere, going inland, the flat road stretches off towards those snow-capped peaks. It's so flat that it silences me. It silences Gordie, too. We've turned a bit quiet, but it's a comfortable quiet that says, I suppose, we're at ease in each other's company. We're very different people, differently wired, but we must have come to terms with that all those years ago, as you do. But we're guys perhaps of an old-fashioned sort and we're not much into open self-examination.

I've got the map out. I want us to go have a look at one of those mysterious lakes that lurk out in Southland's far west not too far from here, where Fiordland rises up from the plains and the roads all stop and the legends start.

There are persistent stories of exotic and even supposedly extinct creatures living in Fiordland's unexplored and vast vastness. There are said to still be moose and mountain lions there, the descendants of animals released long ago for hunting purposes or maybe just for the hell of it. No one's reported any mountain lions in the century or so since the poor things were let go here, but rumours of moose are heard every few years.

There were 10 North American moose liberated at Supper Cove in 1910 in the hope of developing a herd of them in Fiordland, but they supposedly died off due to the precipitous and exceptionally wet and rugged conditions, and the well-established red deer outcompeting them for food. Only a handful of photographs of the doomed moose exist, taken between 1923 and 1953.

Then in 1994, a moose-obsessed biologist called Ken Tustin began putting movement-sensitive cameras in the bush on animal trails near Dusky Sound in the hope of proving that they had somehow survived, but eventually even he gave up the hunt. Which isn't to say there aren't still moose loose in those misty wilds.

And it's said that there might be moa living there still, though I'm not sure anyone really believes that. And of course there's the lost tribe. Or should that be Lost Tribe? They're supposed to be descended from remnants of the earlier Southland tribe Ngati Mamoe, who were decimated in a series of savage battles with Ngai Tahu that raged through Rakiura (Stewart Island) and the coast near Riverton then north and west to Lake Te Anau, where Ngati Mamoe were finally utterly defeated and the few left alive disappeared into the forests of Fiordland. It's a very good legend, though not much informed by actual sightings or, indeed, much in the way of fact.

Fiordland might be even less inhabited now than it once was. Captain Cook visited in 1773 and went home raving about all sorts of things he saw, including the large number of seals along the shorelines. There was a big demand for seal fur at the time, and so sealers soon after followed to slaughter the creatures by the thousands, though sealing wasn't for softies.

Parties of men would be brought in by sailing ship, rowed ashore and abandoned at various points on the lonely, rain-drenched coast and islands in the area, and left to subsist, hunt and be picked up with their skins later. There was a very lucrative trade with China. So lucrative that it probably didn't matter much if men were mislaid and sometimes lost altogether.

There were few accurate records kept at the time. It is known that one group was left to fend for itself on some small islands off Rakiura for seven years. And doubtless some of those rugged and profoundly smelly sealers were never seen again.

One story that is known a little, though it has fallen into legend and even inspired a novel, is about James Caddell, who, as a 12-year-old ship's boy, was taken by Maori when he went ashore on Rakiura with a sealing gang. His shipmates were clubbed down in an ambush, killed, cooked and eaten, but the boy was spared because, in the confusion, he'd accidentally touched the cloak of the chief, Honekai, and, as a result, become temporarily tapu.

Also the chief's beautiful niece had her eye on him and, to cut a long legend short, Caddell was taken in by Honekai and his people, married that maiden, Tokitoki, learned Maori and was tattooed with a moko.

He rose to be a sub-chief of some sort after bringing European skills to the iwi, teaching them to grow vegetables more suited to the climate than kumara, and how to handle a musket. He also joined with them in raids against sealers and, it was said, in the cannibal feasts that were often the outcome in those times.

But, after a time, Caddell was caught between his two cultures and was tempted back to his white side when he became convinced he'd be better off trading with the captains of the ships that were increasingly visiting the area rather than living the old violent man-eating way.

Caddell and Tokitoki went off on one of the ships for a visit to Sydney. He came back to the south to work as an interpreter for flax traders, but perhaps his past caught up with him because Caddell disappeared from the historical record after a last sighting in 1826.

The little-known landmass that lurks on the maps labelled as Fiordland takes up about a third of the whole of Southland, but it's not the same as the rest of the place. After all the flatness of the part of the province where people live, Fiordland is a shock to the senses, a weird cold jungle, all mist and mystery and so hilly it might stretch to Africa if you laid it flat. But there have always been bits you can poke your way into, though you only ever get into Fiordland a little way. You can drive through to Milford

Sound and get a sense of its otherness, or you can drive up some of the roads around the edges that go into the place a bit. They all stop, though.

We've decided to go up the road to the closest of the Fiordland lakes, Lake Hauroko. I've been here before. It's a spooky place in the middle of a beech forest at the far end of a narrow gravel road that runs for 20 kilometres with road warning signs that keep repeating *Caution Roads Oiled.*

Halfway there, we're swallowed by the beech forest, trees suddenly towering above us on either side of the skinny road, the sky reduced to flashing glimpses of blue, the road behind us lost in swirling dust. This one's the southernmost of the Fiordland lakes. From the top, there's Te Anau, then Manapouri, Monowai, Hauroko and the hard-to-reach Lake Poteriteri.

Today's lake is New Zealand's deepest. Carved out by a glacier, it's almost half a kilometre deep, its bed reaching below sea level, which is an unsettling thought. Also unsettling, on its edge, there's a signpost warning boaties of sudden storms. The land around here was a burial place for Maori way back, and there's a bit of a vibe about it, if you ask me.

The lake appears like a dream through the trees at the end of the long gravel road. There's a faint scattering of tourists in the car park talking about the sandflies. We wander down through the trees to the water where the only sign of life is standing all by himself on the jetty. Finally, Gordie has someone to talk to.

This bloke's not a tourist. He's an extremely rugged-looking individual, a possum trapper, it turns out, loading up his little tin runabout with his traps and supplies for a few nights alone in the trees way up there around the bend at the far-off far end of Hauroko.

The sandflies don't bother him, he says. 'But I'll tell you who they like most,' he tells us, though we didn't ask. 'They love English women.' He goes into some detail. It seems he's a student of the impact of sandflies on tourists. 'It's that pale skin of theirs.'

The possum trapper is in good spirits. He says it's a good time to be a possum hunter. 'Seven dollars fifty a skin at the moment. All the ladies are wearing the furs.'

Like Dump Rat, this joker's a bit of a ghost from the past. Even his camping supplies look ancient. 'I wonder what he does out there all by himself at night,' I say to Gordie as we drive back through the forest. I didn't see a book in his box of stuff. Maybe he plays the banjo and

sings to the trees, though I didn't notice a banjo either. It's like driving out of a dream.

Down the road a bit at the old Clifden Bridge, there's a long-drop toilet with paper in it. The one among the trees at Hauroko didn't have any. 'I'd have driven faster if I'd known,' says Gordie with a big laugh, knowing I don't like talking about such things.

The old stone bridge at Clifden doesn't carry the road anymore, but the muscular Waiau River still runs under it, big and sinewy. On we drive through Ohai, an old coal-mining town that has seemed half-dead for years now. There's no retail at all anymore and few signs of life, though people do live here. I just saw a curtain move. Ohai gives me the shivers, a Stephen King sort of place.

In a somewhat similar style, here comes Nightcaps, which, even on a sunny, still, blue-sky day, looks challenged

by circumstances. Someone I used to be married to lives here, which makes me a bit watchful, though we don't have any issues that I know of.

It's just that I haven't seen her since sometime last century, and I wouldn't want to run into her suddenly in her hometown. One of us might have a heart attack. 'I think she lives on this street,' I tell Gordie, who finds it highly amusing. He knows her. She used to work at *The Southland Times* when we did. She was the Lady Editor for a while. That's where I met her. She's a little bit older than me. She'd left the paper before I joined and had gone off somewhere and then come back again, which is when we got to know each other a bit better.

She's in one of those old photos of our parties. A pyjama one, I think, though I wasn't going out with her at the time.

I'd heard she moved here to Nightcaps with the man she married after me. We split up in 1979. Her new husband's a nice guy. I'm not sure what attracted them to Nightcaps, though I should imagine you'd get quite a bit of bang for your real estate buck around here.

Like all these fading Southland settlements, Nightcaps used to be a happening place once upon a time. It started turning into some sort of town between the 1860s and 1880s after Maori workmen employed by the local white overlord, Captain John Howells of Riverton, found a coal seam in the bed of the nearby Wairio River and began using the coal to warm their cold nights in their sod huts, poor sods.

In the late 1870s, the seam was prospected and found to be a major one, coal miners began arriving, and Nightcaps was born, named for the oddly shaped range of hills nearby. With the help of its own swiftly constructed railroad, the Nightcaps Coal Company went on to tear one and a half million tons of coal out of the ground.

By 1900, there were two underground and two open-cast mines being worked by more than 100 miners. To celebrate its success, the company transported a 9-ton block of coal from its mines to the Christchurch Exhibition of 1906. But by the 1920s the easy coal had run out and the once-bustling company town, draped so attractively over a low hill, began its slow and unstoppable decline.

Mines opened down the line at Ohai, the Nightcaps Coal Company wound up, and then the rail line through to Invercargill closed in January 1926. Nightcaps had grown into a proper town by then. There were streets of homes, hotels and boarding houses, a bakery, a butchery, a brewery, a brothel and shops and schools, sports clubs, even a little hospital. And churches, of course.

After most of the mines at nearby towns closed, too, a few decades later, Nightcaps became more of a farming town, but there were bigger and more prosperous farming towns in the district, like Winton, not far down the road, and soon there were no longer the families to live in the tidy streets filled with miners' cottages and wooden houses set on generous sections.

Now the place is on its way to ghost-town status, with fewer than 200 inhabitants, quite a number of them elderly. There is still some coal being mined, but it's a highly mechanised process now and doesn't offer many jobs. The town centre has only one living shop, a Four Square general store, and the Railway Hotel, which has finally been painted, but no railway of course.

I'm not entirely sure why, but in recent years I've developed a bit of a thing about Nightcaps. I'd almost always drive out there on any trips I made back south. I

got so worked up about Nightcaps at one point that I even started working on a novel I set there, which, strangely enough, opened with two friends driving south from Queenstown on a road trip together.

Like some other writers of non-fiction, I have harboured the ambition to drop the 'non' bit, but it turned out to be harder than it seemed to move into a land free of facts, unbound by the actual truth of the matter. At times my non-fiction had drifted towards the colourful edge of reality anyway.

In the 1990s I had a bit to do with Barry Crump, who gave me some advice on writing once which went something like (try and imagine his deep rumbling voice here): 'There's what happened, there's what could have happened and then there's what should have happened.' Barry was suggesting, I think, that a writer run with the 'should'. I'm not so sure about that, but I know what he meant.

In my great unfinished, and possibly unpublishable, novel, there's a chapter set in an Invercargill of the future, inspired I think by a smattering of facts and a sense, at least, of what could have been.

## A NOVEL IDEA

Vim van der Haarden was a familiar figure on the streets of Invercargill, and had been since he moved there all the way from Holland with his chiropody business and his chiropodist wife, Vanda. They set up their practice behind a big sign downtown, upstairs in Tay Street. The sign said Footsy. Vim thought it was cute. He felt he had an ear for English vernacular. Invercargill had not previously encountered such a thing as chiropody, never mind a company called Footsy, and wasn't sure what to think at first.

But despite the slightly alarming sign, the word swiftly spread about the wonders Vim and Vanda would work with verrucas and in-grown toenails, and business became brisk for the van der Haardens, who also made friends easily.

They were a good-looking couple, tall, slim and golden-haired, both. They hosted dinner parties in the large home they bought in the well-to-do part of town. The house backed right onto Queens Park, with its sweeping walks and huge old trees. There was local gossip about the couple's dinner parties.

One night, and maybe more, went the talk, there was a sleepover for the dinner guests. Several couples, all drunk and bedding down together. There was little detail, but much speculation, though sexual shenanigans were nothing new to Invercargill. The climate and the meaty, oystery diet encouraged such things.

No one was surprised when, a safe eight years after settling there, Vim put up his hand for the mayoralty. He'd been a hard-working city councillor for two terms, and had long been forgiven for his Dutchness and his dangerously attractive wife. Their twins, who were now three, had softened the couple's image, too. Now any sleepovers were for children.

Holland, famously, was a land of bicycles, and Vim and Vanda brought their bikes with them to

Invercargill, having read of the Southland capital city's famous flatness. Cycling was a well-established way of getting around the town before the van der Haardens arrived.

The children of the city cycled to and from their schools, a treacherous business in the chilling winters when black frost invisibly coated the streets and footpaths. Adults, though, disdained bicycles, preferring the cosy interiors of motor vehicles, usually large ones.

Until Vim and Vanda arrived, the only grown-up regularly riding a bike in Invercargill was the local loony, Lionel Belsham, who cycled the city's inner streets after midnight applying ominous religious graffiti to fences and lamp posts. He had a model church attached to his bike's carrier. It was a church of his own making, in every sense.

'Don't call me mad,' he'd tell anyone who suggested such a thing to him. He had a certificate of discharge from a mental hospital he'd spent a decade in. He carried it with him at all times and he'd produce it and wave it about if he was angry enough. It was his certificate of sanity. 'Where's yours?' he'd shout.

Later, when cycling had become the very thing by which Invercargill defined itself, Lionel would claim that he'd led the way. But it was Vim who had had the vision.

'Every town has a motto or a symbol,' he told the council when he was a fresh face at their meetings, going on to explain that Invercargill's should be the bicycle. He had some figures about the potential for tourists on bikes and how it could reduce the region's carbon footprint. He produced a drawing of a billboard saying Invercargill: The Cycling City.

'Settle down, Vim,' said old Bill Turner, but some of the others thought it wasn't a half-bad idea and they voted some money for Vim to produce a report, which he duly did. There was no stopping him by then. He was a man with a mission.

Invercargill had experienced previous mayors of vision. In recent years there had been Tim Shadbolt, who had set out to boost the city's shrinking population by dropping fees from the local tertiary educational facilities, bringing a flood of budget-conscious students to the area. Many of them were Asian, a new cultural experience for the locals.

But the population continued to shrink. There was no stopping the people from leaving. They wanted something Southland couldn't give them. The only noticeable gift from the Shadbolt era was a disproportionate number of Indian and Chinese eating places downtown.

Gordie, on the other hand, isn't much drawn to the mystery of Nightcaps, the town or the unborn novel, and loses interest in the place after failing to raise a laugh by pretending to spot my ex-wife, whose name is Vanya, on the street. I start to feel that it would be a good thing to get him out of town, just in case he starts investigating, like he did back in Colac Bay.

So we leave Nightcaps behind and, drive on, north across the great flat land, then east. We make it back to Invercargill after what has turned into a long day on the road, Southland being that bit bigger than we remembered. 'The problem is,' I announce, 'that the places are so far apart.'

'That would be the problem,' says Gordie, rolling his eyes at me. I feel I might have perked up a bit since the little smoke I sucked on back by the Clifden bridge. But we are a little introspective today — and tired, too, by the time we get back to the Kelvin at five.

I've emailed through a request for a meet-up with Mayor Tim back in Invercargill. 'Nothing serious,' I tell his people, 'just to say gidday.' Gordie's keen to meet him for some reason and keeps mentioning it. I know Tim a little from years back in Auckland where he was mayor of somewhere else — Waitakere City, as it was then.

Gordie and I are talking about maybe going to Stewart Island tomorrow, which would make a change from all this driving. Southland, as mentioned, is turning out to be a bit bigger than we remember.

And, before we know it, here we are back in the Editor's Cut with Allie, 'hello, darling', behind the bar and a pint of Emerson's pilsner off the tap. We have a few of those and then dinner upstairs with the same waitress as last night. She says she knows me from somewhere I'm not sure I've even been. Gordie has the lamb and drinks a bottle of chardonnay; I have a steak and drink more beer. Later we go into the house bar and ask for the best cognac they have, and they do have a few to choose from as it turns out.

This hotel seems strangely over-staffed. Morgan was my 'turndown attendant' tonight, according to the note he left on my pillow, which he'd fluffed up. He'd also turned on the annoying standard lamp I can't figure out how to turn off. Never mind, good night, though I won't sleep for a bit yet. There's a line looping round my brain, keeping me awake.

'I don't want to talk about dead people,' Gordie had snapped at me earlier after I started talking about someone who happened to have died. We were out on the Kelvin smoking balcony. Gordie with his Benson and Hedges, me with the calming weed, though perhaps it made me talk too much again. Never mind.

One of the dead people I could have mentioned, and who I have been thinking about since being in Invercargill, was a man called Frank Stapp who I knew here in the 1960s and early 1970s when I was doing the music writing for the *Times*. Frank was an old guy by then, Invercargill's very own version of a New York impresario, a remarkable character who called everyone 'Master' to save having to remember our names. In turn, he became known as 'The Master', though I used to call him Frank.

He brought shows to town, usually to the Civic Theatre, and he'd been doing it since the 1930s. Frank had handled everyone from Louis Armstrong and Laurence Olivier to PJ Proby, Acker Bilk and the ballerina Margot Fonteyn.

It was Frank who'd brought The Rolling Stones for that concert Gordie and I went to. He was protective of all his stars, and if he was ever asked what the Stones had got up to when they were in town, he'd say, 'Rascals, Master, rascals.'

Frank also brought wrestling and circuses to town. He was built on the same lines as Jack Grimaldi, stocky and ancient, always in a suit, an overcoat in winter, wreathed in cigarette smoke, ash often spilled down his front, enthusiastically talking up the act.

'Good house tonight, Master,' he'd say with a smile. He organised his show business life on the side from his day job, as you might in Invercargill, where the stars didn't exactly pour through. Frank worked as a guard with the railways and did the shows in his spare time.

He loved the business, the stars, the sparkle, and he was a good man, straight as a Southland road and, as a result, much loved and respected in the entertainment world.

Frank helped me organise my own show once, at Invercargill's Orange Hall. We brought the singer Shane and a band called The Dedication down, 'direct from Wellington', as we said on the poster, and added a few local acts. I don't recall making any sort of profit, but it was certainly part of my ongoing education, and it was interesting to be on the other side of the game.

Frank used to meet me in the house bar at the Kelvin, buy me a few drinks and encourage me to do a story about his next act coming to town. It didn't matter who or what it was, Frank was always a believer and, unlike many of his entrepreneurial tribe, always made a point of catching the performance. In fact he'd caught so many performances, he once woke up at a church with his wife, Rene, clapping, thinking he was at one of his shows.

He was devoted to Rene, who'd been a ballet dancer. They didn't have any children, and when she died in 1982 it was said his heart broke. He became reclusive after his loss and spent his last years isolated. He turned down a QSM and died in his eighties in 1993.

I seem to recall Frank enjoyed a drink, and once, perhaps spotting I was having trouble keeping up with the steady pace of my companions, advised that there was nothing that settled a drinker's nervous stomach like an occasional crème de menthe. It was odd advice, but I must have needed it.

If I had my way, I'd replace that soldier statue on top of the Boer War Memorial with a statue of The Master, though, being a discreet man, it's not what Frank would have wanted.

# WEDNESDAY

Gordie is shouting at the local drivers through the windscreen. 'The streets are too fucking wide,' he bellows, as if the streets of Invercargill are a new experience to him. He had the mince on toast for breakfast at Zookeepers again, and it's made him lively, especially when coping with the local driving style, which is hesitant and unpredictable.

The locals stop at the stop signs at the tops of side streets, but then they drift out as if they haven't seen us coming in our great blue Falcon, like maybe they're going to hit us. Then they pause again, and then they drift. It's as if all the flatness of land and the wideness of streets has struck them slightly silly.

We're on the road south to Bluff, low light, under a dull, cloudy sky, slow rain falling. There's the fertiliser works I took a job at during some school holidays. I'd decided around that time that I might like to work in a laboratory one day. I think it was an aesthetic thing, after I'd seen a *Frankenstein* movie at the Majestic. I wanted a lab coat and bubbling test tubes.

But I lasted only three or four days at the fertiliser works lab. I caused a spot of bother when I dropped a big glass bottle of hydrochloric acid all over the lab floor on the first day, and then it turned out there was so much fertiliser dust in the air that it made me sick and I was sent home and never returned, turning my back on dreams of a career in chemistry forever.

I share this touching personal tale with Gordie, but I'm not sure he's listening. All that mince can't be good for him. He's probably having to concentrate on digesting it.

We're running quite early for the 11 o'clock ferry to Stewart Island, but we're both chaps who don't like to run things late and, anyway, we want to mooch around dear old Bluff a bit. Though when I say 'dear old Bluff', I'm not entirely sure what I mean. Bluff is one of those places that's a little hard to love from the outside, unless you're the broadcaster Marcus Lush or the poet Cilla McQueen, both quirky types who moved to Bluff from much easier places.

Cilla used to be the partner of the painter Ralph Hotere. I met her here in Bluff when I was directing a TV documentary about her for a TV book-show series called *The Good Word*. She seemed a lovely woman, a poet of course, and therefore a little away with the fairies. She never really explained what she was doing in Bluff, a fragile creature like her in this tough, cold port town.

She confided to us that she'd got to the point of not caring if a poem was even published. She wondered if they ever needed to be written down at all. It could be that Bluff did that to her.

I know Marcus a little, too, and worked with him years ago when we were panellists together on a TV advice show called *How's Life?* He's the sort of guy you don't have to talk to very much to get a lot out of, and I got the feeling at the time that he thought *How's Life?* was as silly as I did, neither of us being entirely clear what we were doing there, posing as TV stars dispensing wisdom on TV to people with problems.

It was the early 2000s, and working in TV was a bit of a pushover at the time, so I was getting all sorts of work, though I was always slightly happier behind the camera than talking to the thing.

*How's Life?* ran five evenings a week on TV One for a few years, fronted by Charlotte Dawson, a loveable, high-voltage ex-model with enormous breasts. I only mention that because she used to have to wear two bras to keep them contained when she was on camera getting excited and waving her arms about.

I was one of the regular panellists, along with Marcus and all sorts of people who've gone on to all sorts of things. It was a powerhouse of fame-hunger and, to add to the weirdness, there was also all sorts of shit going down behind the camera, too. Again, it was an educational experience and it paid okay, too, but I never really fitted in.

Paul Henry, Robyn Malcolm, Christine Rankin, Suzanne Paul, Peta Mathias and Jude Dobson all fitted in, though the others used to pick on poor Jude a bit for being swotty. I wasn't swotty, but I was likely to say anything when a camera pointed my way and it was my turn to give advice to the mother worried about her dope-smoking son or the teenager with the boyfriend problems.

One of the strange side-effects of being on TV, though, is that it never quite goes away. Old programmes pop up on obscure channels in the middle of the night years later and, without warning, you're getting stopped on the street for the inevitable 'I've seen you on TV, haven't I? What was that Charlotte Dawson really like?'

I thought Charlotte was a lovely person, but what did I really know? She seemed a bit broken, like some otherwise thoroughly likeable people are. That had happened before I met her. She'd been a famous model, and that's not an easy thing to grow older with. She was bloody good at the TV presenting thing. A natural, bright and funny.

Bras apart, I was in awe of her, and she was a hoot in the green room and even more fun in the changing room. But she had a fatal attraction to celebrity and, in the end, it killed her.

I worked with Marcus a couple of times on more sensible TV programmes before he moved down to Bluff and away from TV and into radio, which he could do from far-off, which I think he liked, being a slightly faraway sort of guy.

On a visit to Bluff a few years back, I looked him up and we lunched together at a restaurant next to one of the Bluff oyster factories. Mainly, and sensibly, the menu featured oysters, lots of oysters, and they'd cook or not cook them any way you wanted. I recall we ate them at least three different ways that day, and then we went for a drive to some of the hidden places Marcus had found. He was delighted about living in Bluff.

The oyster restaurant's gone now, and I'm not even sure if Marcus is in Bluff much anymore. He was so enthusiastic about the place he ended up buying two houses in the town. He bought the second one, he told me, because he didn't like it when people came to stay and they'd be just down the hall from him. With two houses, they could be just down the street instead, he said.

When I was a kid growing up in Invercargill, Bluff was the nearest place the locals could be a bit snooty about, being only the port town, a drive down the road, the place you went for the ferry to Stewart Island on the school holidays, an older, tougher town, as port towns can be in New Zealand.

It had the enormous Ocean Beach Freezing Works, the province's oldest meat factory, a booming oyster and fishing industry, a busy port, and the ferry to 'the island' as we called it.

It had three pubs along the main drag at the port's edge, and a regular rail service to Invercargill. The school train, bringing the kids to high school in the city, was infamous locally for the riotous behaviour of the Bluff kids. It was said that youngsters were regularly thrown from the moving train.

The other thing about Bluff is that it was home to Southland's most notable density of Maori population and, as a result, the town had an otherness about it.

It still has, though Bluff has had to weather hard times in recent decades. The great haunted castle of a place we pass on our right on the way into town is the old freezing works, which shut down years ago, and the port is half shut-down, too. It doesn't do the trade that it used to do.

There's no hiding Bluff's bedraggled air, the unpainted houses on the streets stretched up and across the great north-facing bluff that Bluff itself clings to, a bit like a stubborn old barnacle. The first Pakeha trading post was established here almost two centuries ago, with the blessing of the locals.

A man called James Stewart, a sailor and ex-soldier who claimed to have fought at Waterloo, was its founder. A tall, powerfully built bloke, he married a local woman, earned the name Timi Katoa or 'Jimmy The Strong', and made a living growing potatoes and cattle. He died at sea aged 56.

In those days, Bluff was called Old Man's Bluff Point, for its landscape, but that was eventually shortened. There was a mad attempt at one point to change the name to Campbelltown, in honour of the family of the wife of the governor of the time, Gore Brown, but the locals took no notice and Bluff it remained.

We're playing a song called 'Drug Time', a wickedly catchy tune by a band on Gordie's road-trip record called Babybird. We're driving up the towering brow of Bluff Hill where the wind is sharp and icy. It's almost too cold to be out in it, but we park and climb the steps to the top and the big view back. The monument stone here has what looks like Japanese lettering painted on its back, and tiny graffiti next to it boldy stating *There's No Whales Here*. And underneath, *Fuck Off*.

Gordie captures the insult with his phone cam and tweets it out to his twittering flock. *Appalling grammar. Bluff Hill*, he captions it. He has a thing about bad grammar.

Back down in the town at a homely café on Bluff's main street, they're offering venison pies, oyster pies and even

mutton-bird pies. Not the sort of thing to eat ahead of a ferry ride across Foveaux Strait, perhaps the country's most challenging body of water.

Gordie's still full of mince anyway, and quite taken up with his expanding tweeting notoriety, endlessly on the lookout for a new photo opportunity to feed his thrill-hungry followers. There are few photo ops as we hang around the ferry terminal, though we do attract unwanted attention with the wet-weather gear Gordie thoughtfully brought with him from his office and which prominently features the TV3 logo.

'Are you doing a story in town?' people keep asking. Our replies vary.

'Sorry, can't talk about it,' I tell someone, trying to look mysterious.

The ferry is $130 return and an hour each way in a big catamaran, a bit like the Waiheke Ferry. Bluff looks better from a distance as we whip out of the harbour and into the strait with 13 passengers aboard. It's nearly 50 years since I was last on Stewart Island, which suggests I'm an older person than I feel.

There was no catamaran then. There was a proper ferryboat, though when it was mutton-birding season the birders would commandeer it and take it off to be a floating hotel while they hunted, leaving the rest of us with the dirty old Bluff tug for transport. It was a bad thing, I remember, crossing Foveaux Strait in a storm in that tug. It used to fill up like a swimming pool.

Ahead of us, that great big misty hulk of an island called Stewart is looming up at us. The sea's fairly calm today, which is a lucky and wonderful thing. Many times when I was a kid, it wasn't.

Back then, my mother and father and my brother and I came sometimes to Stewart Island for the school holidays. It was a magical time and such a haunting place that later I used to wonder if I'd dreamed it: the dripping bush, the fish that seemed to jump out of the sea onto our hooks.

We'd go over there with another family we were friends with and rent what was always described as a 'fisherman's house', usually a neglected and damp old wooden place in the bush, no electricity, long-drop out the back somewhere, full of spiders.

The men would stay the weekends, then go home, back to work in Invercargill, and we'd amuse ourselves hiking about in the bush, fishing from rocks, and being taken out on the boats by fishermen the adults had got chatting to down at the pub. We'd come home sometimes to find scuttling sacks of crayfish left for us at the front door. I had a pet crayfish for a while, though that ended badly.

It was here that I had my one and only taste of kereru, New Zealand's highly protected native pigeon. The trees used to be creaking with them, and someone we knew shot a few and shared them around. Delicious.

Our ferry cuts its engines as it glides into Halfmoon Bay and docks with a swirl at Oban, Stewart Island's only town, only settlement in fact. It seems sort of the same as I remember it when I last saw it in the 1960s, still gazing out at the sea from under its great bushy eyebrows.

There are a few new buildings, ugly utilitarian-looking things, and a big practical tin barn of a community centre looms over the place, but the settlement seems not much bigger than it was in the 1960s. The permanent population then was around 350, and now it's 380 or so, a bloke on the wharf tells us.

We haven't come to stay, though. We've really just come for lunch and we're booked on the 3.30 ferry back to Bluff. Oysters, we thought, would be the taste treat to have, given that oysters from Foveaux Strait are the local food of legend, along with the crayfish and the blue cod, of course. Not to mention the Southland lamb, except we're out to sea for lunch, so it's oysters and maybe crayfish, as long as they're not trying to charge big-city prices here.

First thing, we drop into the South Sea Hotel, which sits up in the little town like a grandstand to the view. We want to check the menu and the seating arrangements, but they're out of oysters apparently. I'm a little disappointed, but Gordie is indignant. 'Good God, man,' he shouts at the nervous bloke bearing the bad news. 'We've come all the way from Wellington for your oysters.'

Faced with this tsunami of outrage, the man behind the counter tells us to try the guy at the pie cart around the corner. The pie-cart guy gets his oysters from the island's other oyster farm, he tells us.

So off we go around the corner, though there aren't many corners in Oban, to the pie cart, which is called the Kai Kart and is painted a blue that's a hue or two brighter than our Falcon. Gordie recognises it immediately. 'I'd know that pie cart anywhere,' he says. 'It's the old Gore pie cart.' And now that he mentions it, I think he's right. I recall its long lines, though back across the sea in Gore it was painted a sober white.

But the Kai Kart's got its *Closed* sign up and there's no one about, though that's not going to stop Gordie, who's now set on a holy mission to find oysters on Stewart Island.

The Halfmoon Bay Museum is the next notable building along the sleepy street, and Gordie's straight in the door and telling the old guy behind the counter about the shocking situation with the oyster supply. The museum attendant doesn't seem to know what to say to this appalling news, and, after a bit, it seems a good time to get Gordie outside for some air.

But the museum man, having collected his thoughts a little, comes out after us. The Kai Kart is indeed the Gore pie cart, he confirms. It was shipped over here and is owned by a man called Jim who actually does have his own oyster farm, not the one that supplies the South Sea Hotel. Museum Man even comes up with a phone number for Jim.

Gordon rings Jim immediately, but the news is all bad. Jim's oysters are spawning, which means that today, against all odds, Stewart Island is an oyster-free zone. This is a terrible development. 'We'll just have to settle for the crayfish I suppose,' I tell Gordie.

Gordie sighs. 'I tried,' he says.

We wander back down to the South Sea and its dining room with a view, where we order two servings of salmon trio, locally caught, delicious, and two $40 crayfish, generous, cooked perfectly.

Beers, cheers, then we take a lunch-settling wander back up over the western headland behind Oban to Bathing Beach, the birds zipping above our heads between the great wedges of bush that line the road. Bellbirds, tui, kereru big as chooks, flying around us like we don't matter at all.

Gordie's a bit out of breath on the hill. Taking a break, we pop into an old wooden Presbyterian church on the hill above Halfmoon Bay. Gordie asks a passing woman, a tourist who's been here a week, to take a photo of the pair of us on the road outside on the hill. We tussle about who's going to stand on the short side of the picture. I lose.

The sun's out now and it's warming up considerably. We take a seat in the shade out in front of the Four Square, Gordie all taken up with his burgeoning tweet audience. He tweeted the mutton-bird pie and the photo of the *Fuck Off* from the top of Bluff Hill, which has gone a bit viral he reckons.

Back down on the wharf waiting for the ferry boarding call, Gordie gets chatting — as Gordie does — to a man decanting diesel from a whacking great tank of the stuff,

the island's supply. The power generation is still all diesel-fuelled here. Alternatives have been investigated, the diesel guy tells us. It's too windy for a wind farm, too cloudy for solar, and too sparsely populated and far away from the mainland to go to the trouble of running a cable across.

They might get hydro one day, from one of the island's rivers, but hey, when's tomorrow? The man with all the power talk is a Cockney. He's been on Stewart Island 14 years. We don't ask him if he's ever homesick. He doesn't look the homesick type.

Back on the 3.30 ferry to Bluff, we're sunburnt and stuffed full of crayfish. Aside from the bloke steering and his mate standing by, the crew on this ferry are all women, strong, husky young women hauling big mooring ropes with a confident air. I feel uncommonly safe and, with a few bounces from the boat, we're back in Bluff, sparkling untypically in the December sun.

On the drive back to Invercargill, we get talking about some of the bits we don't know about each other, like what got Gordie wanting to be a newspaper reporter in the first place. 'I was a bumptious little shit, but one thing I did know was that I didn't want to be a farmer,' he says. 'I had the full suite of farming skills, but the work was too repetitive and too hard. I quite liked haymaking, but I did not like shearing. I remember working 'til midnight and being so tired I was crying with exhaustion. So no, I didn't want to be a farmer, though I'd have made a lot more money, I suppose. I was good at English at school. I won the sixth form English prize. I was dux twice.'

'Settle down,' I tell him.

'Well, I was,' he says. 'I had an inquiring mind and I was a big reader. People kept telling me I was good with words. My Grandad Tom knew someone at *The Southland Times*.'

But Gordie says he went first for a job he'd seen advertised at the local radio station in Invercargill as an advertising copywriter. They gave him a test when he went for the interview, he says scoffingly, asked him to write 100 words about the wonders of oranges.

'That's a bit weird,' I tell him, because I, too, went for that job at the local radio station and I, too, was asked to write something zesty about oranges and, like Gordie, failed the audition.

'I took the piss, I think,' he says.

I don't recall what I did, though I know I didn't have much to say about oranges.

My high-school career was a little less glorious than Gordie's. If my education was a line on a graph, it was going downhill at about 45 degrees towards the end at high school. The vocation officer said my best chances of employment were a choice between teaching, being a librarian or maybe a journalist, which didn't really seem any choice at all. I went home and wrote my first letter to the editor of *The Southland Times*.

Oddly, I still have that letter and the follow-up one I wrote, along with the editor's replies, not because I sentimentally kept them, but because they came back to me. Twenty-odd years ago a new editor at the old paper was having a clear-out of bits and pieces in the filing cabinet he'd inherited and found those schoolboy letters of mine, along with Gordie's, tracked us down and posted them back to us.

'Heaven knows why they were kept', he said in his covering notes to us. It was April 1967 when I wrote the first letter, a rather reiterative follow-up to that meeting with Mr Grimaldi. My handwriting is clear and calm, something I couldn't manage now. It also seems to seethe with a confidence, or perhaps that's just desperation. 'Dear sir,' I said.

You may remember I spoke to you recently regarding a cadetship in journalism with your newspaper. After giving the matter serious consideration, and having discussed it with my parents, I now wish to officially apply for a cadetship.

I am sixteen years old and am a sixth-form pupil at James Hargest High School. I passed School

Certificate in history, geography, general science and English at the end of last year. I also hold a Chamber of Commerce certificate in arithmetic and English ...

This year for University Entrance I am taking history, geography, biology and English.

I have always been interested in taking a career in which I can use English and as I enjoy writing I thought of journalism.

I have never been actively interested in sports, perhaps because of my lack of ability in this field, although I do belong to a golf club at school.

I have always enjoyed reading, my choice of books is varied and I prefer reading books with a little depth. Having no particular preference for an author I shall give you an example of what I am reading at the moment, *Bleak House* by Dickens, *Brighton Rock* by Graham Greene and *Uhuru* by Robert Ruark.

In my spare time I like to go fishing or listen to modern music. I also like going to dances and to the cinema.

If you feel I should remain at school and attempt to gain University Entrance before applying for a cadetship I would be prepared to comply with your wishes.

Then, only a week later, after I'd received a letter back from the editor promising that they'd hold a vacancy for me, I wrote back, cheeky little prick ...

I am grateful to you for your prompt and gratifying reply to my application for a cadetship in journalism. I

shall, as you advise, strive to attain University Entrance
and will contact you at the end of the year.

I neither strived nor attained University Entrance in the
end, but by the time the results for the exams came out it
was too late. I'd already started work with *The Southland
Times*, and I must have been doing something right because
they kept me on.

Thomas Gordon McBride, on the other hand, arrived at
the paper after the shearing season of 1968, having sailed
through UE — getting an extra $2 a week for that, I found
out later. If I'd known that, I might have tried a bit harder.

On our way back into town, we search Invercargill's
southern suburbs for the house Gordie had bought as a
newly married 19-year-old father-to-be. When we were
flatting together, we'd had a brief flirtation with forming
a rock band. I bought an electric guitar, Gordie got a bass
guitar and a great big bass amp. We'd play along to records
and make a terrible din, but that was about as far as it got.
Anyway, we never found a drummer.

'When I got married I swapped my bass amp for a
wringer washing machine,' says Gordie. 'I gave it to the guy
in that band A Gentle Feeling. Remember them?' I do.

'And I sold the Mini and got a bigger car. Reality kind of
crashed down on me. Life had been kind of carefree before
that,' he says. 'It was so carefree, I didn't use a condom.'

But Gordie can't find the street he used to live in.
All the old houses look a bit the same and, after driving
around and around for a while, we head home to the

glorious Kelvin for our third episode of *Groundhog Day*. Back over the inevitable cleansing ales in the Editor's Cut, the conversation picks up and we swap tales of disastrous dates, one-offs. Mine is about the time I took a nice Catholic girl out for dinner. I don't know why I remember she was Catholic and, anyway, that hardly turned out to be relevant.

'I think Sheryl might have introduced me to her,' I tell Gordie. 'I must have been nervous and trying to impress her, because I took her to that upstairs restaurant down in Esk Street, the Las Vegas.'

The Las Vegas was a classy place by Invercargill eating-out standards in those times, offering chicken in the basket, various sparkling wines, and even a small dance combo in the corner on Friday and Saturday nights. The date was going swimmingly — the chicken in its basket, the icy Corban's Cuvée in its bucket, my glittering small talk. We might have just ordered Irish coffees. I offered her a ciggie. I believe I smoked Peter Stuyvesant in those days. She took the proffered fag. She looked lovely by the light from the candle, one of those round red numbers that burns down inside itself.

In what I probably thought was a French-movie moment, I picked up the candle in its holder from the table and leaned across with it to light her cigarette. But the bloody candle wasn't stuck on its little spike properly and as I held it up to her fag, the treacherous red candle rolled forward and deposited a good half-pint of molten wax straight down her cleavage and all over the front of her nice frock. I don't remember the sound she must have made. It's one of those memories you self-erase. I took her home. There was no goodnight kiss.

After several days of my ringing and pleading for a second chance, she finally agreed to a lunch in some candle-free zone, but I slept in on the day of the date and didn't turn up, which was the end of that. Anyway, she was possibly a bit posh for me. 'I don't think she came to any of our parties.'

'Not all that many girls ever came to our parties,' says Gordie.

His disastrous date story involves a girl parked up with him in the legendary Mini in the rural backblocks somewhere near Wyndham, necking in some farmer's drive. 'We were going to go all the way,' he says, 'then we decided it was a bit public. But it had been raining and the Mini got stuck. I had to get her out to give the car a bit of a push, but I spun the wheels and sprayed her head-to-foot with mud. That was that.'

Both stories are liquid-based, which is interesting. I give up on my beer-only ethic and we lash out and order a bottle of $82 Central Otago pinot noir to go with my steak and his venison. It's all a bit hazy after that: the smoking balcony, the sun still not gone completely from the sky as I fade out.

But not before thinking about Gordie and what a helplessly engaging person he is, fully endowed with that nosey old reporter thing that I can do, too, but with him it's natural, an instinct that kicks in the moment he encounters anyone at all. Everyone really.

Dunedin tomorrow will be a whole other thing. Maybe it's Southland that binds us. Up there will be new territory, somewhere we haven't previously been together.

Gordie told me tonight about his brother and sister, who are younger, and how none of them wanted to stay and work the farm, though their father understood. His sister lives now in upstate New York, his brother has a vineyard in Marlborough and makes a particularly good rosé, according to Gordie. It's good that someone does.

# THURSDAY

Here's that cold wind again, nosing down Kelvin Street as we fight our way along and around the corner to our usual breakfast spot with the animal statues. Gordon's one of those people who starts lively, kind of like a motor-mower. I'm more subdued first thing. Maybe second thing, too. 'It's going to be a great day,' he shouts, ordering his mince on toast for the third morning in a row.

Somewhere out on the road late yesterday, I got a message from the Invercargill mayor's office offering us a meeting with Mayor Tim at nine this morning, but Gordie has lost interest in meeting the mayor and we've decided to skip out on that, so I email my apologies and turn Tim down. 'He should have come to see us,' says Gordie. 'And bought us a beer in the Editor's Cut. It's the very least he could have done. I'm actually feeling a bit insulted.'

We're in no rush at all to get to Dunedin. First, we're heading to the vast, sparsely populated eastern stretches of Southland, to Gordie's tūrangawaewae, out Wyndham way. But we're going there by a roundabout route, first out

towards the coast. There's cow shit on the road out here. The clouds hang low.

As we near Fortrose, whitebait shacks are dotted along the big, lazy river. The only living things to be seen are the sheep dotting the fields. Houses seem, at first glance, to be abandoned, but there are lights on in some of them.

We take the road out to Curio Bay. Gordon stops for a photograph of the sign for Dead Horse Road to tweet out to his burgeoning band of followers who can't get enough of his rural observations. His following has now hit three figures. I don't say it to him, but I don't think there's anything remarkable about a road in New Zealand called Dead Horse. It seems Gordie's followers are easily excited. They're mostly city types, I suppose.

It's a bleak old day out here. We pass another dead dairy factory. Southland is littered with them. In the old days,

every second little country hamlet across the province had its own dairy factory. Now and then when I was on my school holidays, I'd go with Dad to work and sometimes accompany him on his regular calls to little dairy factories across the province where he'd talk to the men in charge about stainless-steel tanks. We'd always come home with some free cheese, often an enormous round of it. His favourite was blue vein, which was probably a bit exotic in those days.

Here's a signpost for Otara, which is not like that northern one at all. In truth, it's not much more than a sign really. We hang a left towards Waikawa with Warren Zevon singing 'Splendid Isolation' in the car, which seems appropriate in this neck of the woods.

We park up at Curio Bay, where the southerly's coming off the surging ocean in great blustery gusts, and come across a pair of tourists, from Washington State, they tell us. Gordie, the inveterate connector, gets gassing with them, but really they don't have anything of interest to say.

At a little store tucked away back in the tussocky dunes, there's a blackboard outside announcing *Today Is Milkshake Day*, but that mean wind is whistling another tune.

Gordie says he had his first-ever swim here, and there is a beautiful beach down there below us, a caramel-coloured curve. But this is not swimming weather, and we didn't bring our togs anyway. We're back in the car, warming up, chasing the dusty roads, cutting across the southern edge of the Catlins, zig-zagging the narrow ways back towards Wyndham, which is a way inland from the coast, deep in sheep country.

We stop at Waikawa, a one-horse hamlet notable mainly for a roadside display of petrified wood from a nearby slightly famous petrified forest. A piece of wood-turned-to-

rock is displayed behind a large sign stating, without any detail, *Petrified Wood*. 'A stranger might think it just got a terrible fright,' I say to Gordie, who photographs it for his followers. We give it a caption: *Was it the axe?*

The only other thing of note in Waikawa is a little old wooden church. Just that, the petrified wood and all that sky. People around here must have fantasies about hills. And on we roll to a place called Niagara where we stop for a coffee at its café, a hippie haven of a place in an old school house. It calls itself the Niagara Falls Café, which we feel might be pushing reality a bit.

Gordie decides to take the matter up with the management. 'Is there a waterfall around here?' he demands of the young man behind the counter.

'Technically,' says the young man. That's not a good answer. Gordie glares at him and demands detail. According to Mr Niagara, there's a bit of a creek just down the road, and in that creek, if you search about a bit, there is actually a small waterfall. Quite small. Not worth signposting or anything. Gordie frowns and decides against having a coffee or even a slice of the ginger crunch, which does look tempting.

On we go, up a back road through the Waikawa Valley and the rainforest, which lines this twitchy, narrow slip of a gravel road. The trees have been trimmed vertically so that each side towers like a great green wall, 15 metres or more above us. Then we're out into a sweet, undulating, open valley, following the Wyndham Stream, Gordie pointing to this and that as the memories come back to the old farmer's boy.

This is deeply rural. A muddy, narrow road, sheep, low cloud clinging to the hilltops. We're getting close to Glenham, south of Wyndham, where the McBride farm was. Still is, in fact, though it's not the McBride farm anymore.

'See that shed there?' shouts Gordie. 'I helped build that.'

'It's a barn, Gordie.'

'Nah, it's a shed.'

And here's the old McBride homestead, a big wooden villa dating from the late 1800s, proud and freshly painted atop a hill behind its trees. The McBride family farm ran to 600 acres, mostly grazing sheep. They were good years when Gordie was growing up. 'Wool was a pound a pound,' he says. There was a billiard room in the house. Gordie's mum played piano. They all sang.

There are no McBrides here now, and of Glenham there are only remains — an old church and the peeling shell of the Glenham Store. 'There used to be an old slaughterhouse over there,' says Gordie, 'down from the primary school. It had the biggest rats I've ever seen. The farmer laid concrete to keep them out, but they ate right through it.'

On we go, north towards Wyndham, over the hills, high enough for us to look out over all those little places rolling south of us. There's the super-sized new dairy factory at Edendale, way off in the misty distance. It's as big as a castle.

In quiet Wyndham town, Gordie's on a promise to his mother to visit his Uncle Bruce, who's 90 and living in the local rest home. He finds the rest home and parks outside. 'You don't have to come in,' he tells me. I don't like being left behind.

'Shouldn't I come along and take a photo of the two of you for your mum?' I ask.

'Nah. I'll be only ten minutes.'

But Gordie's back in five. It turns out that all the oldies have gone down the road and they're having lunch at the Three Rivers Hotel, so we drive down and Gordie pops in there for a quick hello to his old Uncle Bruce. Wyndham is a bit of a shadow of its former glory, but we're not finished with it yet.

Gordie, on some sort of nostalgic roll, drives us to his old high school where, as he has mentioned several times, he was dux. He reckons there must be some sort of plaque on the wall here mentioning all the glorious former duxes. He reckons his name will be there somewhere. I had the opposite sort of high-school experience, so it's hard to take this sort of talk too seriously, but I try not to show it.

Sadly, there's no roll of honour. It turns out that someone burned the old school down years back and they built a new one in the same spot. The arsonist was local. Everyone knows who it was, a teacher tells us, but the police didn't have the evidence to charge him. The teacher even tells us the name of the road the arsonist lives down and we spot it on our way out of town.

Gordie's spur-of-the-moment school visit causes quite a fuss in the staff room. We're given an impromptu tour of the school, even though it's not actually the same one Gordon went to. There's a swift search of the school records, but of course a lot of stuff went up in smoke, thanks to that unarrested arsonist down the road.

If we went down to the museum, we might find something, we're told. 'They'd love to see you, too, Gordon,' says one of the teachers. But we don't do that. Instead, we scoot back through town and out the other side. 'I bought my first joe at a shop just over there,' says Gordie, a misty tone in his voice. Joe, meaning condom. I haven't heard one called that in a long time.

'Does the name come from GI Joe?' I wonder out loud, but Gordie's not listening. Instead, as we head west towards Highway 1, for some reason we get to talking about the pension, which will leap into our pockets within the year. The fucking pension. 'Who ever thought?' I ask Gordon. There's no answer to that.

Straddling Highway 1, Mataura is as Southern Gothic as ever. Sadly, they've diminished the effect slightly by taking down the scary, peeling old sign just off Highway 1 right by the bridge with the picture of the man in the river with his rod. It was a bit unsettling, I suppose, but I miss it.

This town is still the spooksville of the south, though. It could have been otherwise. The cascading falls on the river might have made an alluring town centre if they weren't instead spilling down hidden behind the awful, old, stained rears of the meat works and the paper mill.

Even though the paper mill closed back in 2000 and the freezing works is now a slick and modern high-tech killing operation, there's an evil-coloured liquid glooping out of one of the many pipes in the backs of the buildings and down into that famously trout-filled river. Adding to the drama, the Mataura River runs an unsettling reddish colour, though that's just the iron oxide from the ground around here.

There's a sign outside the Four Square advertising *Marlow's Pies — the Healthier, Tastier Choice*. There are lots of trucks. There's nothing about this place that makes me want to pause and eat a pie.

But once it was otherwise. Mataura was quite a place, a hyperactive hive of industry, in fact, a centre of major assorted factories arranged around that once-lovely river and its falls. The town that grew up around the falls was called just that at first, The Falls, but then it became the name of its river.

Maori had long come to the falls in pre-Pakeha times to harvest the lamprey they called kanakana, a delectable fatty eel-like creature with a sucker-shaped mouth that it uses to climb the rocks at the falls.

Near here, in 1836, the last great South Island Maori battle was fought when a war party of Ngati Tama and Te Ati Awa jumped a Ngai Tahu village at Tuturau and slaughtered everyone they could get their hands on.

Then, as the attackers slumbered, bellies full of kanakana and the flesh of their victims, a Ngai Tahu relief force attacked, did a great deal of slaughtering, and re-took the village.

Then the white man came south and messed up the river with a tannery, a sawmill, a meat works, a flourmill, a dairy factory and a paper mill. It was here, on the banks of the increasingly brutalised river, that the paper mill produced New Zealand's first manufactured paper.

They could make only brown paper at first, and then the mill was swept away in a flood three years later, in 1878.

But then they built a new mill that could make white paper, too, and soon the heart of Mataura was a noisy, smoky, pollutey industrial zone full of great chimneys smoking with coal torn from the nearby open-cast mines.

A bridge was built across the then quite-mighty falls, but when the cascading water cast too much spray onto the bridge, annoying the locals, the falls were dynamited, shortening their rise and destroying their grandeur. And then the bridge was washed away in another flood and the local government built the ugly concrete one that just made us shudder.

And now all the ugliness is for nought. The flourmill was knocked down in the late 1800s to make way for the freezing works. The dairy factory closed in 1980, and then the paper mill shut. But there was a time when Mataura roared, though not in a particularly loveable way.

Up the road, Gore bustles, a bit like Winton bustled, but much more so. If a country town has enough heft, it lives on while the smaller towns around it wither. Gore is such a place, seeming alive and really quite well. There's cash in this town. You can feel its pulse. The cheese rolls are good, too — at the Café Ambience, three for $7. That's pretty good value, and for quality I'd put them slightly ahead of the Kingston ones.

While we're at the café I pick up the local paper, and I'm surprised to read that some ratbag or ratbags unknown have burnt down the Riversdale Swimming Pool. A difficult thing to do, I would have thought.

Parked in the main drag, the mighty Falcon is sheathed in so much dust and dried mud that we have to open the doors carefully, for fear of soiling ourselves. When we slam the boot shut, a cloud rises.

Despite its rural reputation, Gore is quite an elegant town, mostly flat, established in 1862 and named after one of New Zealand's lesser-known governors, Sir Thomas Gore-Browne. Hopes for the settlement's growth were so extreme in the late 1800s that for a while Gore was referred to as the 'Chicago of the south'.

And while that turned out to be a little optimistic, the town did boom quietly right through until the 1970s. Then farming took a nosedive, Gore shrank, and businesses, including the town's landmark cereal mill, closed, though it still stands. Then, come the turn of the twenty-first century and the dairying boom, Gore was back in business.

Adding to its patina of elegance, Gore is home to an arts-and-heritage precinct, one that actually lives up to its claim, if only for the rather surprising Eastern Southland Gallery. Housed in a curvaceous old brick building, the town's original library, it's smack in the middle of Gore, just a few steps from the place's defining artwork, the giant vaulting statue of a brown trout, where the road turns to cross the river, which is, apparently, just teeming with trout.

The building the gallery's in was designed by ER Wilson, the architect who also came up with Invercargill's most notable landmark, the Invercargill Water Tower. If on the outside the gallery's all curves, then inside it serves another curve. Aside from a major collection of works by Ralph Hotere, it houses the mad and wonderful John Money Collection.

Money was a New Zealander who lived out most of his life in Baltimore. He was a psychologist and a sexologist, as well as being an avid art collector who gifted his formidable, resolutely catholic and slightly loopy collection to the good people of Gore.

There are paintings in here by Theo Schoon, American Lowell Nesbitt, a lovely series of moons over London by Rita Angus, some vivid Aboriginal art, and a roomful of eerie, larger-than-life wooden figures from Mali.

Money, who was moneyed, bought art not because he loved each piece necessarily, but because he wanted to support the artist, though that can't have been the case with the African figures, which look ancient and unsettling, the sorts of things that might come alive after midnight. Money must have had a particular thing about those. Maybe it was something to do with the sexology.

John Money was an interesting guy, a bisexual bachelor type who was born way north in Morrinsville, but spent most of his life in America, where he cut out a remarkable and surprising career for himself.

He moved to the States in the late 1940s to study psychology at Harvard, and went on to run the disturbing-sounding Psychohormonal Research Unit at John Hopkins University in Baltimore, where he made his home in a converted corner shop in a rough part of town.

Unbeknown to most of New Zealand, Money made quite a name for himself in America. In his intimate investigations, he had a similar curiosity to the likes of Kinsey and Masters and Johnson, and, like them, he was a target for outraged response to his groundbreaking work in the intimate areas of the human condition.

In the 1950s and 1960s he became involved in the treatment of children who were born hermaphrodites and, controversially, he was one of the founders of a sex reassignment clinic, offering parents a surgical solution. He set up a research unit for the treatment of people with sexual disorders, and worked with sex offenders.

He wrote dozens of books and hundreds of papers across the whole panoply of sexuality. He wrote about sex for *Playboy* and *Cosmopolitan* magazines, chatted on *The Oprah Winfrey Show*, lectured on the topic of 'Pornography in Homes' at John Hopkins, and routinely screened hardcore sex films to better educate his wide-eyed medical students.

The feminist writer Gloria Steinem and the exploitation moviemaker John Waters were big fans of his. Hone Tuwhare wrote a poem for him. He was one of Janet Frame's early therapists. And Gore, of course, should forever be grateful.

Money's mad and wonderful collection ended up here in Gore by sheer accident of connection, when Jim Geddes, the man who now runs the Eastern Southland Gallery, was travelling across America in 1989, visiting various galleries and museums.

A friend of Jim's asked him to look up her Uncle John if he happened to go to Baltimore, and Jim did visit Baltimore, and Uncle John turned out to be John Money, who showed young Jim his remarkable collection, which by this stage was crowding him out of his house. They made a connection and they kept in touch.

Then, in the mid-1990s, when Money decided to downsize and began trying to find a home for his collection, he remembered the enthusiastic young curator from Gore and, to cut a long and circuitous story short, ended up gifting the lot of it to the far-off Southland town, where it now awaits astonished visitors.

Just across the road from the Eastern Southland Gallery, there's the Hokonui Moonshine Museum, a slightly more predictable sort of installation, though only slightly. It's a shrine to the great spirit of the south.

It was the poor quality of the whisky being sold locally that supposedly drove the mid-nineteenth-century Scots immigrants in the area to start making their own hooch. By the time the imported stuff reached Gore, it was often watered down and probably a pretty low-grade drink in the first place.

This caused particular distress to a formidable Scottish woman called Mary McRae, who had come to settle in the hilly Hokonui district, west of Gore, with her seven children and a long experience in making whisky back home in Scotland. Amid the luggage she brought to her new home was a box marked 'household goods'. It contained a small whisky still, which she schooled her sons to use.

By day they worked hard clearing bush from their block of land. Mary McRae served as a midwife for the area, which was said to be like a little bit of Scotland transported. Gaelic was commonly spoken by the locals, the pipes were played for entertainment, and a dram of whisky was taken with the morning porridge and probably at regular intervals during the day.

The old lady lived into her nineties and credited her daily dram for her longevity. And she and her sons didn't sell their stuff to just anyone, apparently. It was said that you had to 'have character' to be allowed to buy McRae's whisky.

Gore's Moonshine Museum has a licence to distil and sell the stuff, made to the original McRae recipe, which it offers in bottles with a skull-and-crossbones label. It tastes just about as rough as that moonshine my school friend's dad used to make in his backyard. Southland, as mentioned earlier, has had a long and troubled history with the demon alcohol. Like Invercargill, Gore has a licensing trust.

Just south of Clinton, the sky lightens. We've run out of CDs we want to play again. We only brought two each, and my ZZ Top one turned out not to ever quite fit the mood. The fields along the roadside are filled with innocent lambs and their daggy-arsed mums. Clinton itself seems mostly closed. There's never been a great deal to say about Clinton, except that it's about halfway between Invercargill and Dunedin. You'd only stop here if you had a puncture.

To entertain ourselves we resort to fantasy and invent a new sports team for the south, which we decide to call the Southern Reticence, though we're not sure what sport they'd play.

'They wouldn't say anyway, if they were asked,' I tell Gordie. 'They're reticent.' All the regular sports are taken in any case.

'Maybe they could play competitive parking,' I make the mistake of suggesting. It gets Gordie raving again about the driving habits of southerners.

'Have you noticed,' he asks rather forcefully, 'that the parks on the streets are actually longer down here, and they still can't fucking park properly?' I had, as it happens, noticed that the parking spots were longer than usual. Everything, bar the population, is bigger down here.

Apart from our natures, one of the things that marked Gordie and I out from each other when we met up all those years ago was our choice of transport, though I'm not sure I had much of a choice in mine. He certainly did. He came to town driving his own car, and not just any car but a Mini, light blue with fat tyres and a larger-than-standard (he still likes to point out) 1100cc engine.

I, on the other hand, was getting about on the best vehicle I could afford, a spearmint-green Vespa motor scooter, which could possibly have been trendy had I been in London or Brighton, where I might have posed as a mod. But there were no mods in icy Invercargill, only rockers, and there was no such thing as trendy there in those days, and perhaps not even in these days.

I might have been the owner of the only motor scooter in town. Invercargill was a motorbike town, after all. It had its own motorbike gang, those Antarctic Angels, who favoured big, noisy old English bikes like Nortons and BSAs. They'd laugh openly at me as they roared past, or more likely they roared openly at me as they laughed past.

But they never ran me off the road. Anyway, I was pretty good at doing that all by myself. Every now and then, when one of our parties was petering out and I was feeling like I'd never ever get a girlfriend, I'd ride drunkenly to the outskirts of town and see how fast I could make the

Vespa go down the first country road I could find, ears freezing in the frosty air until the road usually ran out and I hit a wire fence and went flying into a field. Once I came around a corner a bit sharply and ploughed into a great pile of gravel out of sight on the shoulder of the road. That was an interesting sensation. But despite my best efforts, I never did myself or the Vespa any lasting damage.

Gordie only ever crashed his Mini once, he reckons, and it was all the fault of his raging hormones. 'I had a girl with me. We'd been at a barbecue down by the river near Wyndham, and I must have been a bit keen to get us somewhere else, because I rolled a tyre off on a corner and went off the road. The girl was a bit shaken, but the car was okay.'

There was another notable night starring Gordie and that zippy Mini of his — and me and Pauline Sutton, one of

our fellow reporters from *The Southland Times*. We'd been having something to eat at the pie cart down the road from the office when there was some sort of a run-in with some fellow diners, rough redneck guys. Gordie recalls it involved steak, eggs and onions and 'some sort of splattering'.

We had to make a run for it, jumped in the Mini and took off, but the rednecks made chase with bad intent and a much bigger car. Luckily Gordie's driving skills were too much for them, and, despite a few close calls in cul-de-sacs around some of the newer suburbs of Invercargill, we escaped when the bad boys finally spun out and hit a lamp post.

'I saw it happen in the rear-vision mirror,' says Gordie, with a smile at the memory.

Gordie loved driving. Once, when the first-ever Kentucky Fried Chicken outlet opened in Dunedin, he says he drove there and back from Invercargill to get some of the new taste sensation that was sweeping the nation, though not quite sweeping as far as Invercargill at that time.

'And once I drove from Invercargill to Nelson, had a walk around and drove home again,' he says. I wonder if Gordie's Mini is still out there somewhere. If it is, it must still be catching its breath.

Gordie just loved travelling actually. Once, he set out from our flat in Invercargill on foot and hitchhiked up and down the whole country. There's an old photo someone took of him in Hamilton to prove it.

Here's Balclutha with its big river, crossed by its ugly ferro-concrete bridge. It's just like the bridge in Mataura, but

with a lot more arches. Balclutha is named, of course, for the full and fearsome river that runs through it, the Clutha, New Zealand's biggest. It, in turn, is named for the Clyde River in Scotland, Clutha being Gaelic for Clyde.

Balclutha's not famous for much aside from flooding, but then the town's asking for that, hanging around a river that's famous for that sort of thing, going right back to the beginning of Balclutha, which is South Otago's main centre of commerce and what passes for civilisation in these parts.

In the great flood of 1878 the house of a local carpenter and his lady friend was hit by a huge floating log, which lifted the house from its foundations and sent it off down the river. The carpenter, a German, enterprisingly ran around inside to keep the house upright. I'm not sure what was his lady friend did. Sat tight, like the carpenter probably told her.

Eventually someone heard their shouts for help, took out a boat and rescued the pair shortly before the house was swept out into the breakers at the river mouth and torn apart.

Even after that and the floods that followed regularly over the years, arguments to move Balclutha were ignored, and here the place sits to this day, just waiting for its next big wash day.

There's a sign to the side road for Kaitangata, an old coalmining town with the most dangerous place name in New Zealand. It's South Otago's version of Southland's Nightcaps, an old coal town whose embers have long cooled off and half the previous population, and more, departed.

'Kai' does mean food and 'tangata' man, but the name might just mean that this was a place where a man might find a decent feed. Though there was a nasty battle here in the 1760s when the invading Ngai Tahu defeated the local Ngati Mamoe and then feasted on them, quite a common story in these parts.

With the arrival of the white settlers, Kaitangata grew slowly as a small river-port town from the 1860s, then it boomed a bit when high-quality coal was found nearby and mines were put down to pull it out and cottages built for the miners and their families.

One of the other notable things about Kaitangata was the great mining disaster of 1879, when 34 miners were killed in an underground explosion caused by a build-up of methane set off by a miner wandering in with a candle. Still, it's all history now. The nifty new-looking sign on the outskirts of the not-so-lively-looking town declares *Kaitangata — Black Gold Town*.

The church is closed for business, but there are two stores and a pub. Smoke drifts from a few chimneys. The old dairy factory, long-abandoned, sits in a sea of dead cars.

Milton, the next notable settlement once we're back heading north on Highway 1, is another town that isn't quite what it used to be. Milton, as the name quietly suggests, was a mill town, though some claim the place was named after John Milton, the English poet. Either way, now the old mill stands long-abandoned, half-hidden in the trees by the river on the outskirts of the flat little old town.

Milton moved through the whole gamut of milling from the mid-1800s on, first with flour, then oats, and then, most famously, with textiles at the Alliance mill, mostly all over now. There are a couple of other interesting things about Milton. One is that, for no apparent reason, there's a sudden kink in the otherwise straight stretch of Highway 1, halfway through town. And another interesting thing about Milton is that it's where Martin Phillipps grew up, Martin being the gifted singer/songwriter and founder and ongoing leader of The Chills, perhaps New Zealand's best-named rock band, still operating in their ninety-ninth line-up.

Martin has long lived in Dunedin, where The Chills formed, still working on his masterpiece, doing the occasional show with a band of younger players now. There was a time when he and a different set of Chills very nearly made it to the tippermost of the toppermost of the pop world. Well, the alterative pop world, anyway.

They were lauded by the critics, including me, they toured the world, recorded albums in exotic places, their songs were on the radio stations, and even tickled the underbellies of the charts. But despite lots of wonderful songs, Martin's pop bubble didn't burst so much as never quite fully inflate, which hurt him I think.

Once, after a particularly good royalty payout back in the 1980s when it was all happening for the band, Martin bought himself his dream car, a beautiful old Rover. He took me for a drive in the country in it one afternoon when I was in town, to interview him maybe. I can't recall if we made it to Milton.

Right now there's a sign on the edge of town that says *Milton — Town of Opportunities*, and I hope someone got paid well for that line, because the person who dreamed that up had a great deal of imagination.

There's also strange imagination on display up the road in Mosgiel, with its showy and inappropriate Hollywood-style sign, but that's quickly forgotten as up over the hill we soar, past the Lookout Point fire station on the left, to the sudden sight of Dunedin below us, magnificent in wind and wintry rain. That sort of weather suits the place. Anyway, it's not weather. It's climate.

Quickly, it seems, we're down in the heart of the old city, in sepulchral Princes Street with all its old buildings and its air of emptiness. We check into the Southern Cross Hotel, which used to be the grand old hotel in town until it changed its vibe a bit by also becoming Dunedin's casino.

In a change of arrangements, the hotel has upgraded us from the interconnecting tower suites I'd booked and into their presidential suite, which is splendid and multi-roomed, with two bedrooms, two bathrooms, a full kitchen and a dining room. Gordie immediately celebrates by taking a shower, bellowing and singing away in there like a happy hippo. I lift a beer from the house bar.

We pop across the Exchange to a pub in one of the beautiful old stone buildings nearby, the Duke of Wellington, but it's got the wrong groove, trying too hard to be olde English in an old Scottish city. It's almost empty

and is so lacking in distractions that Gordie keeps sighing, so we leave after one pint apiece.

On the way back, walking up Princes Street, we run into someone Gordie knows, Alan Hall, a TV producer who used to work in Australia. Alan's here working with Natural History, making shows for export. He's with his wife, Silvia. We tell them we'd love to meet them tomorrow night for a drink if they're free. They are.

Further on, after another bar, we take ourselves upstairs in a narrow, old building, on steep Stuart Street, above the Octagon, to a Scottish-styled restaurant called Scotia. For dinner I order a rare and unusual dish, confit of hare, while Gordie eats hogget, the best sort of sheep meat, he reckons. He remains committed to a meaty diet.

We drink drinks. It is all splendid. Life feels good. And it feels even better when, a little later, at our hotel's jangling casino, Gordie turns $100 into $145 at the blackjack table in 20 minutes flat. It's about knowing when to fold them, he says, though I'm sure Kenny Rogers said that first.

More drinks, then bed. Vast bed. Sleep is also vast.

# FRIDAY

I awake imagining there's a water buffalo upset about something in a nearby room, but it's only Gordie at the far end of our vast suite greeting the world with a series of tremendous bellows and honks. Now he's singing something in the shower. He's a force of Nature. On the other hand, I force myself out of bed.

We ordered room service breakfast last night, and sit down to it at the table in our own dining room in our enormous suite. We felt duty-bound to make use of this vast space they've given us. Gordie's breakfast is hearty; mine mostly toast and coffee. We're not sure what to do with ourselves today.

I tentatively pull back a heavy curtain. It's another cloudy, cold-looking day out there. We decide to start with a bit of a wander around town.

Up Princes Street a little way, Gordie spots a barber open for business and impulsively pops in for a trim. 'And do the eyebrows while you're at it,' he tells the man, who does what he's told. I didn't know you could do that. But I tend to go to ladies' hairdressers. Gordie's needs are much more basic these days. He still has a fine head of hair, but he gave up the Beatles cut long ago.

Gordie's keen for us to go to the movies later. There's something on called *Nightcrawler* that he's heard good things about. It's screening at the Rialto in Moray Place, the strange circular street arrangement down in the heart of Dunedin that circles the famous Octagon. There's a mid-afternoon session that might suit, he says.

Meantime, we decide to take the filthy Falcon for a run up the Dunedin side of the harbour to Port Chalmers, the city's ruggedly handsome little port town, its good looks somewhat overwhelmed by its ugly out-sized container wharf. This is where Scott left for the Antarctic, and, on the subject of cold things, from whence the first frozen meat was shipped to Britain.

There's a whacking great stone memorial to Scott up Blueskin Road on the steep hill behind the town, staring out over Port Chalmers and beyond. It's worth going up for a look. It really is monumental, a mighty column with a great stone anchor perched on its top.

But it feels a little early for monuments, so we don't stop in Port, as the locals call it, and roll on around the windy waters' edge, through Carey's Bay and on to Aramoana and the mole, out at the end of the road right on the mouth of Otago Harbour. The mole is the massive breakwater built out there in a bid to control the interface of sea and sand at the mouth to Otago Harbour.

There's a spot around the coast not far from here with a colourful name, Murdering Bay — another one of those southern places named for what it is, or what it one time was. It was there, in 1817, where some murdering was done between sealers and local Maori, though there are various versions of what actually happened, some quite colourful.

What might be regarded as the tabloid version suggests that, as a result of some grievance, a group of sealers was attacked by the locals and three of them killed. The grievance may or may not have had to do with one of the sealers having bought a preserved Maori head down Riverton way to sell in Australia, helping set off a gruesome and lucrative trade in the items.

Anyway, after the first lot of murdering, the sealers came back fully armed and set about killing in revenge. It's said they wiped out a whole village. There are other milder versions of the fatal encounter available, but in all of them there's at least a modicum of murder, hence the memorable name.

Aramoana, with a name that means 'path to the sea', is just a little place, scattered about, half-hidden on the sandy flat. It's hard to approach it without feeling faintly guilty for being here, that we're only here nosing about because of the village's dark and lasting fame after that madman David Gray went on his shooting spree in November 1990, killing 13 people before charging out to his own death in a hail of police bullets.

On first approach, we drive on through Aramoana to the road's end and park up out on the edge of the Otago Harbour mouth, looking right across the powerful water to the hulking peninsula on the opposite side. Gordie gets talking to a couple of divers getting set to slip off the side of the old sea wall to explore the wrecks of three ships down there, sunk to help hold the wall against the great surges of the water here. There's a cold wind blowing, though the divers don't agree when I mention it. 'A great day in paradise,' says the talkative one, as the talkative ones tend to say.

There's no shortage of shipwrecks to explore round this coast, one of the most famous being an old Spanish slave ship with an unlikely name, the *Don Juan*.

The ship had come to Port Chalmers as the *Rosalia* in the 1870s, in such a sorry state she was refused a certificate of seaworthiness, stripped, anchored permanently and used as a shipping office before being towed to nearby Deborah Bay and sunk. Shackles to hold the slaves had been found in her hold, and her earlier name and her history in the human trade discovered.

In Aramoana, a shy, closed-faced collection of cribs and dwellings, we spot something surprising — what looks at first to be a pirate ship posing as a house. That house is definitely ship-shaped, and there's a skull-and-crossbones flag on a mast and a hippie-looking guy mooching about in bare feet out the front.

We slow down, I lower the window and say gidday, and Gordie and I get out and wander over for a chat. The hippie, exceptionally friendly, introduces himself as Doi and even spells it for us. It's his ark, he says, nodding at his house and inviting us in for a look around.

It's extraordinary indoors, with a hand-hewn wooden interior with lots of detail and a faintly Hobbit-ish vibe, but sensibly full-sized. There's something called a 'Wishing Booth', though we can't have a quick wish because Doi says there's a ceremony involved to make it work properly, with

dancing and the waving of ribbons. Gordie and I aren't that desperate to make a wish.

We meet the hippie next door, Margaret, and several laidback dogs. They're sweet, dreamy people. But there's a good reason for Doi's place being an ark. It's built on nothing but a spit of sand, and the whole of Aramoana is barely above the level of the sea, which is, famously, rising. Living in an ark makes a lot of sense. Doi's plan, when he saves up enough cash, is to coat his ark house in ferro-concrete, make it watertight and, when the time and the tide finally come, just float.

It turns out that Doi, like Gordie, was born in Riverton. Doi drifted up north a few years back. A bit too far, he says. 'I moved into a commune up in Golden Bay, but it was too hot,' he says, so he came back south, but not all the way, to Aramoana.

There are dangers for Aramoana besides all that rising sea out there. The towering cliff face that rears up massively on the hamlet's western edge is studded with enormous boulders poking out of the softer rock and mudstone like giant cannon balls, revealing a little more of themselves with each downpour or little slip. Some of them look ready to roll right down to the road far below and maybe even on through a crib or two, or even an ark.

Some boulders already have come thundering down. There are dents in the road where they bounced. But Doi doesn't seem troubled by the thought of bouncing boulders or rising seas. He shows us his going-to-town gumboots, cut down into shoe shapes. Town is probably Port Chalmers of course, not Dunedin, which might be a bit racy.

We decide the only thing that makes sense after Aramoana is for us to drive all the way around to the other side of the harbour, right over there across the water, on the Otago Peninsula, to the village of Portobello, for lunch perhaps.

So it's back through Carey's Bay we go, pub on the right, set in against the cliff. It must lose the sun shortly after lunchtime. There used to be a whacking great Ralph Hotere painting hanging in the bar in that pub. Hotere, back when he was alive, lived just down the road in Port Chalmers.

Half an hour on, under a suddenly sunny sky, we're way out on the other side of the harbour, opposite Dunedin on the peninsula road, which wriggles around the northern side of the great peninsula, just a lick above the water line.

I grew up just over the hill from here in a suburb called Waverley, in a little brick house my parents had built up there around 1950. Although we moved away to Invercargill when I was eight, I've got memories of this place. I remember the rocky shoreline and this road. I remember being brought down here by Mum from our place to help line the road with other kids waving flags as a big car with the Queen and the Duke inside rolled by. I was about three. Much more interestingly, I remember once catching an octopus off those rocks down there.

Mum and Dad built their first house together up there about the time I was born, a fairly humble place that looked out across a valley to farm fields rising up on the other side. I have memories of kneeling on the sofa in our lounge, chin on the windowsill, looking out at that view, watching the lambs dance their crazy dance at dusk. The farm's long gone now.

The whole of Waverley was a farm once. It was owned by the local minister, the Rev. Thomas Burns, and it was called Grant's Braes, an odd name that was passed on to the local primary school, which I went to until we moved south.

Grant was the Rev. Burns's wife's family name, and a hillside in old Scottish is a brae. There's no shortage of braes in Dunedin. It's a wonder the word isn't more common around here. It's a wonder really the city wasn't called Braetown instead.

The suburb next to Waverley, stretching down to the winding road on the sunny side of the peninsula facing Dunedin, is Vauxhall, named for something that used to be there.

There's little evidence of it now, but in the 1800s, before there was this road that came all the way along the Otago Peninsula, before this part of the city was filled with houses with views, Vauxhall was the site of a half-forgotten and rather odd frivolity, a pleasure garden.

It was reached by a little ferry running back and forth across the harbour from the city. It must have been a surprising new entertainment option in the 1860s for a town full of parsimonious Presbyterians.

Dunedin was founded in 1848 by members of the Free Church of Scotland, who'd fallen out badly with the Scottish Presbyterian Church and come to this faraway place to pursue their own brand of the dry old faith. In the early days, the settlers were mostly Scottish, two out of three of them Presbyterian, and employers advertising for workers would commonly state 'English need not apply'.

Even 12 years after it was settled, Dunedin still wasn't offering much in the way of commodious living, being little more than a scattered settlement with a population of only about 2000. It was, apparently, a profoundly unappealing spot, bereft of sanitation, sun and civilisation.

According to a *History of Otago*, 'The so-called roads which served as thoroughfare for pedestrians, horse and bullock traffic alike, were unlit and devoid of metal, with the consequence that, in times of rain, they became a treacherous morass of miry clay which merited the settlement the name of Mud-Edin.'

Then gold was discovered inland, up in Central Otago, and things changed swiftly as miners, and the merchants, hustlers, hookers and hangers-on who followed the miners, arrived in considerable numbers at the new port. In the last six months of 1861, 20,000 people came in through

Dunedin. In one single day in October of that year, 1500 were recorded as coming ashore at the town's crowded and overworked wharf.

Among the camp followers the miners brought, there were all sorts, some of them of the entrepreneurial variety. One of these was a bloke called Henry Farley. He made a fortune off the back of the gold rush and settled in Dunedin, which, by this time, must have seemed unstoppable.

After a slow start, the 1860s were the boom years for Dunedin. Within a couple of years, the town's population had shot past 15,000 and there was no sign of it slowing. It must have seemed like a kind of madness. In 1860, for instance, Dunedin had five pubs, and by 1864, there were 87.

As the city sprouted, Henry Farley got into retail in a big way. He built shops, a music hall and then a 54-shop nineteenth-century version of a mall called the Royal Arcade, which dominated the town centre and brought the Dunedinites pouring in with their purses.

Farley, by this time a rich man, felt he had a natural instinct for the needs of the locals. He took his biggest punt yet, deciding the new city needed something sophisticated, a marvellous diversion, a pleasure garden like London's famous seventeenth-century Vauxhall Gardens, which had closed just a few years before Farley hatched his grand second-hand scheme. His pleasure gardens would have a lot in common with London's gardens, including the name.

Lacking enough open space in the fast-growing city itself, Farley decided the best spot for his big entertainment venture was across the harbour on the sparsely populated Otago Peninsula. In 1862, he leased 20-odd acres of headland over there, declaring, 'No expense will be spared to render these gardens the resort of pleasure seekers and others in search of recreation.'

Farley then reached deep into his pockets and set about throwing a large amount of money at having the barren headland landscaped and gardens laid out with walks and picnic spots. There were statues and follies, stages for entertainers, a dance rotunda, and swings and areas for various sports and entertainments, a tea gardens, and a vast bar for the thirsty gentlemen, with an adjoining ladies' area.

There was a zoo with vultures, monkeys, an eagle, kangaroos and even some Tasmanian devils. And there was the ferry to bring people across and back to town. The great enterprise caused a lot of local excitement, with the Vauxhall Pleasure and Tea Gardens opening to great fanfare. It was all the go at first, a grand success and a site for many great occasions.

In 1866, a great fête was held at the Vauxhall Gardens with an array of entertainers, including the then-famous English circus entertainer Pablo Fanque, who would have his fame revived a little a century later by The Beatles when they gave him a name-check in their song 'Being for the Benefit of Mr Kite' on their ever-popular *Sgt Pepper's Lonely Hearts Club Band* album. Which makes a strange and unlikely connection with a band that would actually visit Dunedin 100 years later, though they hadn't written that Pablo Fanque song at that stage.

Fanque, who was 70 by the time he played the Vauxhall Pleasure Gardens, was a most unusual figure for the times, an acrobatic black man who'd first visited Dunedin as one of the stars of the Royal American Circus in the 1850s. He was operating a family troupe in England by the time of his return to Dunedin, and made a great impression with his tightrope walking, though the locals were probably quite easily impressed, even by an elderly acrobat.

In the later 1860s, things went downhill a bit, but there was always a somewhat wayward aspect to the Vauxhall Pleasure Gardens. A local newspaper had noted that the 'nooks' and secluded walkways in the gardens went by such names as Venus Arbour and Cupid's Retreat, and expressed concern at such seeming wickedness.

And, over time, wickedness did indeed come, and the Vauxhall Gardens became notorious for darker pleasures and gained a drunken and debauched atmosphere, with prostitutes now offering themselves in its glades and sailors staggering about and peeing in the flowerbeds, not to mention what they got up to in the pergola.

Meantime, the construction of a road out along the Otago Peninsula had made the growing city keen to develop that area for housing and, after the pleasure gardens were closed in 1870, the headland was subdivided and sold off in lots for high-end housing.

And it was named Vauxhall in memory of that old foolishness, though hardly anyone much remembers it at all now. But there are supposedly still bits and pieces of old gateways and arches from the pleasure gardens lurking in people's backyards.

The man who started it all, Henry Farley, died just 10 years after the gardens closed, aged 56 and in sad circumstances, in Sydney, where he was visiting his sister-in-law and her husband who owned a hotel there.

Farley, who had been suffering some undiagnosed illness, went out alone to the theatre one night and didn't come home. He was found by passers-by, collapsed on a city footpath in the early hours of the next morning and taken to the Sydney Infirmary, where he lay, unidentified and unable to speak, for six days before dying.

A post-mortem revealed that an artery in his brain had ruptured. His brother-in-law finally identified him after he read a description in a Sydney newspaper of 'an old man' found on the streets and realised who it might be. Harley was buried, alone with his name, in Sydney.

Meantime, alone with each other, Gordie and I drift on beyond Vauxhall, through Macandrew Bay, Company Bay, Broad Bay, all glittering in the sun. In lovely little Portobello, with its nearby aquarium and albatross colony, we take lunch at the Penguin Café, sitting at a table outside in the sun looking back across the harbour towards Aramoana. It doesn't get much better than this, I think we're both thinking.

'You could get used to this cruising around,' says Gordie as we wait for our pies to come. Gordie's recent tweet of a picture of a road sign for Plucky Street has proved extremely popular. 'That one was always a winner,' I tell him. He's not listening. He's too taken up with his invisible followers. 'Petrified Wood' is also a hit, he says.

Picking up my own phone, I find I've had an email telling me I've got a book deal. 'They seem quite enthusiastic,' I tell Gordie.

'That's great,' he says.

'Up to a point,' I say. 'Now I'm going to have to write it.'

'Don't be so fucking gloomy,' says Gordie.

'You're right. I should just enjoy the moment.'

'You know,' he says, changing the subject utterly, something he quite likes to do, 'I saw my first television here in Dunedin, when I was a kid up visiting some family and they had one.' Dunedin's the first place I saw TV, too. I watched it through a shop window in Princes Street. There was a damp little crowd gathered in the rain staring in wonder at this blue-grey flickering thing that would one day give employment to both of us.

After our pies, on the drive back down the peninsula towards the city, I show Gordie a rugged-looking door on the roadside, set right into the cliff there, just below Vauxhall. It always intrigued me as a kid, and I extemporise a bit of dark local history for him.

The long and winding peninsula road was built, at least in part, by various sorts of prison labour, and some of those prisoners were Maori warriors captured in the Land Wars in the warm far-off north of the country. The cruel guards used to lock some of them in there, I tell Gordie, nodding meaningfully at that grim door.

Gordie's outraged. Beneath that bluff and jolly exterior lurks a seething liberal. He takes several photos, and tweets one out with a wordy caption about hidden shameful history. 'No plaques here,' he adds, leaving me worrying now if I have that story entirely right.

And I don't, as it turns out. I might have the wrong door. There's a welter of responses to Gordie's tweet, one

of them from a local historian pointing out that, though the Maori prisoners were kept cold and miserable as they worked, building the peninsula road, that cavern behind the cliff door I got Gordie ventilated about was probably used for storing explosives, not road workers.

Back in town, we carefully park the filthy Falcon and head off up the hill to the movies. Afterwards, we're meeting with Alan Hall, that old TV producer mate of Gordie's we ran into last night. We'll have a drink or two with him and his wife, then take ourselves off for dinner. There are only two other people in the Rialto for *Nightcrawler*, which turns out to be a nastily clever satire about television and its dark hunger for death and violence, though we already know all about that sort of thing.

In a turn for the slightly surreal, Economic Development Minister Stephen Joyce is now one of Gordie's Twitter followers. 'Good God, Gordie,' I ask, 'who next? John bloody Key?' Gordon now has 226 followers, which might not be an army, but it's a small crowd and a big jump on the 17 he had only days ago.

On our wanders we spot a poster for a Dunedin hardcore music gig starring a band called Foe, supported by Scumhammer, Slitzkrieg and Teeth. Good names, we agree. Gordon wants to take a picture and tweet it, but I restrain him.

'I wonder what Teeth sound like?'

We head down off George Street to a café there for an early beer or two. Gordie mentioned our drinking plans in a text to his mate and TV3 political editor Patrick Gower, who has apparently just tweeted this out to his own battalions of followers, in case a couple of hundred of them feel like popping down for a cleansing ale with us.

Gordie's friends Alan and Silvia join us and we chat. They're a lovely couple and seem fond of my old mate. Silvia asks Gordie, seemingly casually, how he's been keeping, how his health is, like you might just ask someone you haven't seen for a while.

Except maybe they've heard something. I don't know, but it seemed a casual inquiry. 'It's not good,' says Gordie, 'and I don't want to think about it.'

This, of course, opens their mouths and shuts them up again for a bit. Then, the moment Gordie wanders off to the powder room, they're all over me with questions. I think they must definitely have heard something about his health. It seems that way. I tell them a little of what I know and leave it at that. 'I don't think he wants to talk about it,' I say. Well, no.

Alan and Silvia head off home after an hour or two, and Gordie and I move to a table for dinner. The place is packed. The menu looks good. Gordie, ebullient, takes a photo of the young waiter, who looks surprised. He'd better brace himself, because there's more attention to come.

'I'm going out for a cigarette,' says Gordie.

'I know you're not upset about me smoking,' he adds. 'I'm doing it because I can.' He wanders out, which is good timing. Someone in the vicinity has just farted an appalling fart. The diners at nearby tables glare at me as if I'm to blame.

The waiter — tall, husky, tatts, goth-style beard, earrings — looks a bit like he might be the bass player in one of those bands we saw on the poster down the road, perhaps Slitzkrieg. Or Teeth. 'You in a band?' I inquire of him, but I don't catch his answer in the din of conversation and clanking cutlery. I ask if he likes Beastwars, New Zealand's current metal band *de jour*.

It's just that I happen to know Gordie is acquainted with the Beastwars guitarist and the drummer. I wander out to the restaurant patio for a smoke with Gordie. He's pacing up and down with his fag, blowing smoke at the cold sky.

I mention that the waiter is a big Beastwars fan and light a discreet joint, though of course there's no such thing as a discreet joint. 'I know you won't be upset,' I tell Gordie. He laughs.

When I was a teenager in Invercargill, it felt like I was growing up on another planet from the rest of the young world out there around the globe. The rest of the young world was, apparently, tuning in, turning on and dropping out, smoking grass, dropping acid, tie-dyeing their T-shirts and their pillowslips. In Southland, there were severe limits to the things we could get up to, least of all the latest new escape mechanisms for young people, like drugs.

The only drugs immediately to hand were in our parents' medicine cabinets and no use at all unless you had piles or trouble going to the lav. I knew all about the wonders of marijuana and LSD because I'd read about them. I even had a copy of *Surrealistic Pillow* by the Jefferson Airplane, which I'd bought after my high-school Latin teacher, a hip young thing trying to impress us, played it to us in class.

After the rumour went around about what Donovan really meant when he sang that song about 'Mellow Yellow', my mates and I dried a banana skin and tried to smoke it — arrgh. It did make me dizzy, though. But then so did one of the fags I sneaked from Dad's packet.

All we had available to adjust our world on those special Southland social occasions was beer. There were wild experiments with cider, and there was a period when we favoured chasers of blackcurrant nip with our big bottles of Speights. Blackcurrant nip was cheap and surprisingly powerful if glugged in any quantity. You just didn't want to throw up on your nice white Saturday-night going-out shirt after drinking that stuff, though. Well, not unless you fancied having a lilac shirt.

Parties at our flats were never enhanced by mind-adjusting substances of a non-alcoholic sort, though I do recall a friend who was recently back from a visit to Australia coming to a party, smoking what appeared to be roll-your-owns and giggling just a bit too much.

It wasn't until the 1970s and Auckland that I finally got to tune in and turn on and all that. The problem is I've had trouble turning off ever since. And now, after more than 30 years of smoking prohibited natural substances, I sometimes wonder if I might have fried too many brain cells. My memory banks sometimes seem like they've had too many withdrawals. Total recall is often a distant memory, detail a lost cause.

My mood-altering habits may also have had an occasional impact on my judgement. In the mid-1990s, against all sensible advice, I wrote a story about what was headed up 'a life under the influence' for a trendy magazine of the time called *Planet*.

It was a cocky piece of nonsense and I slightly regret letting it out now, though most of it was true. And, on the up side, I suppose, having written it means I can never go into politics.

I was living on the North Shore of Auckland when I discovered marijuana.

# Going South

It was the '70s and the North Shore was a bleak and socially deprived part of town, full of expatriate English with no intention of losing their accents and nervous swimmers with no intention of getting out of their depth. You needed marijuana just to survive the place.

I was working the night shift at the *NZ Herald* and got home regularly at dawn after sessions at the Press Club in the company of alcohol-adjusted cynics and lubricious cadets. It was a confusing time and I don't recall much detail except that the days seemed to last forever and I had only two nights off a week. Those we spent partying.

I don't remember the circumstances surrounding those virginal lungfuls of dope smoke, but I do remember I was driving towards the Harbour Bridge with a carful of crazies when the full effect hit me. It was amazing — so amazing that, suddenly believing I was Jesus on Wheels, I announced we wouldn't bother with the bridge; we'd drive straight across the water to town. One of the crazies grabbed the wheel, stopped the car and threw me in the back.

I'd grown up on Speights back in Invercargill, but I'd moved on to more sophisticated stuff by the time I relocated to Auckland — vodka and tonic, lager, non-fortified wine, that sort of thing. I caught up on the less-legal drug culture later, but once I did there was no looking back.

Marijuana worked fast, made everyone and everything more interesting and didn't deliver a hangover the next day. Also, there was a lot of it about. I recall parties where we passed around Kleensaks full of the stuff, rolling joints the size of salamis and raving all night.

There were side-effects, of course. Dope made you talk more, laugh more, eat more and sometimes fuck more than was rational or conducive to continued personal safety.

Under the influence of marijuana, I thought Stevie Wonder's *The Secret Life of Plants* was a great and cosmic album. But in the '70s the music was mostly so bad we needed marijuana to compensate.

Marijuana also, when you were relatively new to it, tended to make you paranoid. But then that's not necessarily a bad thing in someone red-eyed and raving.

I stepped beyond dope when it was still the '70s. It was at a party in Parnell that I discovered hash and got so crazy I indecently assaulted a national icon.

Whacked out on dope, hash, non-vintage wine and a lot of beer, I lurched to the bathroom in search of much-needed relief. It was a big old bathroom in a big old house and, in my severely adjusted state, I couldn't locate the light switch. It was as black in there as a whale's belly — and about the same dimensions.

I was so crazed I couldn't even find the toilet by feel. I could barely find myself; but I did find the bath and, in my desperation, relieved myself in it. Now slightly less demented, I fumbled my way back towards the door and on the way felt the unmistakable bump of light cord on forehead. I tugged it. Big mistake.

A terrible sight greeted my eyeballs. Anticipating a severe outbreak of munchies among their bent guests, our hosts had thoughtfully prepared a sumptuous supper to be served later. Wanting to keep it cool and out of harm's way, they'd laid it to rest in the bath.

Somehow I'd held steady in the dark and peed on the pav, but nothing else. I made what repairs I could, beat a paranoid retreat and said a polite no thanks to supper.

By the time the '80s rolled around, I wasn't on the North Shore, at the *Herald* or going to parties in Parnell anymore. I was living in Ponsonby where, one year, in a garden not much bigger than that Parnell bathroom, I managed to grow a dozen sturdy dope plants — enough to last us through winter, as well as giving away bagsful to friends.

I was writing columns, interviews and record reviews and sometimes the dope seemed to help with those key first and last paragraphs — though I was always careful around Stevie Wonder albums.

Within a few years I stumbled onto other drugs too and moved to Grey Lynn where the backyard was bigger. But the police helicopters flew as low as mosquitoes and after three straight years of rip-offs by freelance marijuana harvesters, I washed my hands of green fingers.

By the late '80s what had once been pleasures had, as the legend goes, indeed become habits and I was happily putting away a bagful a week. There were

pricier habits available and I had some of those —
notably booze.

But life rolled on and so did the fingers. By now,
New Zealand Green was a match for the strongest
smoke anywhere. Visiting rock musicians keeled over
under its influence or, if they were wimps, diluted it
with tobacco. And over all those years, despite all
those raids by all those police choppers, the price and
the availability never varied much.

Neither did my consumption. I was getting through
a steady eight to ten joints a day, had learned how to
function in public places while under the influence and
somehow held steady in an increasingly unsteady world.

Grey Lynn was gradually falling victim to the wallets
that had previously bought Ponsonby. You had to be
careful about the odours that drifted from your window
— and the police choppers were flying lower than ever.

Recreational drugs had become escape hatches
to nowhere. My friends were turning grey and going
crazy. Fun had become a potentially life-threatening
pursuit.

Increasingly, we were the most out-of-it people
in the room — pub, club, backstage, paraplegic toilet.
Short-term memory loss was some compensation, but
not much. We needed deliverance and none seemed
to be at hand. Until now.

Because now marijuana has become that
unspeakable thing — fashionable. Bands are writing
songs about it and building floppy philosophies
around it. Smoking dope is becoming, good God, cool.

Time to get off. Time, as that great modern thinker
Huey Lewis said, to get a new drug.

Twenty years later, Huey Lewis is history and smoking cannabis isn't that cool at all anymore. Instead, it's medicinal, but then some of us always knew that. Also it helps make you hungry for dinner.

Back inside the restaurant, Gordie drags the heavy-metal waiter into the light so he can get a better photo of him to tweet to his mates in Beastwars, who he has now promised to put the waiter in touch with. Gordie has ordered the duck confit, partly because the menu offers an extra leg for $8, which we agree is a bargain. But, when it comes, Gordie's not a happy diner. He waves the waiter over.

'This is the worst duck ever,' he tells him, and not in a particularly subdued way. 'That's not duck confit,' he elaborates, 'it's deep-fried duck.' There's an interesting new tension in the restaurant and it's increasing. And Gordie's not finished with his food review.

'I've eaten duck confit all around the world,' he announces, 'and this is the worst duck I've ever confronted.' He's breathing heavily. I feel like we're in a *Monty Python* skit. The waiter is in some deep distress now, quite a change from our sweet relationship with him earlier. He must be regretting letting Gordie take that photo.

He suggests Gordie might want to have a little chat with the chef about his confit. 'The other guests, sir,' pleads the waiter. 'If you could keep it down a bit.' Gordon's eyes bulge slightly.

'Is your chef a big guy?' I ask the waiter, concerned about what could happen in the kitchen.

'Smaller than your friend,' he says.

Gordie is winding things up a bit here, but that duck does not look great I must say, more KFC than confit at a glance. And the extra leg at $8 only makes it look worse. On the other hand, my steak's very good. Perfect in fact, though it's hard to concentrate on it with all this tumult going on.

We leave, but not very quietly. The manager takes $48 off the bill, but Gordie's still muttering darkly about the duck. He took a photo of it and tweeted it out. *Not duck confit, Dunedin.*

As we weave through the Octagon, it's packed with revellers, filling up the tables on the wide footpaths outside the bars. 'Look at the beards on those two,' I say to Gordie, nodding at two young hipsters with settler-sized whiskers.

Gordie, of course, insists on taking a photo and the hipsters are happy to oblige. They seem flattered in fact. That's more ammo for the tweet world. We'll caption it *Beardwars.* Dunedin boy racers rumbling through the Octagon in their hot wheels get Gordie shouting, 'Great car!' and waving and snapping away at them with his phone cam. The noisy children rev back in delight.

Back at the hotel, we drunkenly decide to take ourselves back to the casino, mainly to see if Gordon's luck at the blackjack table will hold. Or maybe we just feel like another drink, and who should we run into but Alan and Silvia from earlier, who, like us, are a little turped-up.

Silvia likes the slot machines it turns out, while Gordie drifts back to the blackjack table and comes back richer for a second time, having, once more, known when to fold them.

While our other halves are off gambling, Alan and I drink some bad brandy straight and talk. He used to play drums in a rock band and tells me how much he hates bass players. They're all arseholes, he reckons, which seems an unusual attitude for a drummer.

But then it turns out guitarists aren't much better, and singers, well the less said about singers the better. Then Gordie comes back 50 bucks up and we drink more bad brandy, then, somewhere in the midst of it all Gordon says, 'I'm going to die', and we run out of words to say to each other or the desire to get much drunker.

It's after midnight and we're all older than we used to be — especially after that duck confit.

# SATURDAY

Hungover, we sleep in. There's no movement 'til nine, and Gordie's a quieter boy this morning in his bathroom. We're checking out of the hotel and heading off to Naseby today for some curling and, doubtless, more drinking and eating.

Gordon is Tigger, me more Eeyore at the start of the day. We can switch characters slightly later in the day, but no one — save maybe Tigger — bounces like Gordie first thing, even with a hangover. Downstairs, the breakfast buffet steams alarmingly all along one wall of the hotel's restaurant room.

Gordie stalks the buffet, fully recovered by the sight and smell of it, rubbing his hands in anticipation. There's no mince, thank God. I stick some white bread in the toaster and poke around for the marmalade.

We pay up at the front desk and carefully load the luggage and get back into Old Filthy for the drive north over the hills from Dunedin and then out west across the high country of Otago to Naseby, where we'll spend our last night on the road together.

It's a grey day and cold, as our mornings seem to be. Up George Street, busy as ever, then on the road's big corkscrew at the end, around up and past Pine Hill and onto Highway 1 again north of dear old Dunedin, both feeling slightly the worse for wear.

'Nothing a mutton pie at Palmerston won't fix,' I announce, but Gordie's not so sure.

'I hate mutton pies.'

'These are a better class of mutton pie,' I tell him. He shudders. I suggest we leave Highway 1 over the hill at Warrington for the loop road that goes up through the tiny village of Seacliff and rejoins Highway 1 at Karitane.

I thought I was going to die on this back road once on a previous drive alone to these parts. The road's more of a country lane really, sealed, but narrow as it twists and turns around the edge of the land above the sea on this part of the north Otago coast.

On that trip I came zipping around a corner, not over the speed limit, but at a confident speed because I knew the road, except I didn't know there'd be a dog in the middle of it when I came around.

It was a big dog, a mastiff maybe, and I hit it a glancing blow as I braked. It took off, shrieking, into the bush on the roadside, out of which stepped four or five blokes, gothy types in dark clothes, hoodies, drug-pale faces. They came up and stood around the car, and there was something about their demeanour that suggested they weren't happy about me running over their dog. I had the faint feeling I might be about to be beaten to death.

I lowered my window and offered what I hoped sounded like a sincere apology. Something like, 'Shit, man, I'm sorry — there was nothing I could do.' The nearest one glanced at the others and shrugged, and they disappeared into the bush where the dog had scampered, possibly in its panic death throes, though hopefully not.

It's a lovely drive, though. Seacliff's about halfway along, a little circle of houses out on a headland above the sea and, up the hill, there's what remains of the old and fairly legendary Seacliff Mental Asylum that stood for a hundred years or so, until it crumbled and the main building was knocked down. It was quite a sight apparently, especially if you like your sights a little Gothic.

The building was built in the style of a Gothic 'fantasy castle', which seems an odd thing now, but that sort of thing was all the go at the time. Its design was based on that of the Norwich County Asylum in England and featured a showy 50-metre tower.

Some of the outbuildings still stand, including the old slaughterhouse, because Seacliff had a farm around it where some of the patients worked. Whether those patients were allowed to butcher the sheep and cattle I don't know.

Janet Frame, famously, was committed there. So were two of my distant cousins, who lived their lives out and died in the place. They were sisters and they were born a little to the north, in a sleepy little North Otago town called Hampden.

When Seacliff Mental Asylum was completed in the early 1880s, it was the biggest building in the country at the time, a vast folly of a place housing 500 patients and

50 staff, and so poorly designed that it had more than 1200 doors with individual keys for the warders to lock and unlock, and windows so high in the bedrooms that the poor inmates couldn't even see out of them.

There were troubles with the place all down the years, the worst perhaps occurring in December 1942, when a fire killed 42 women patients who had been locked together in a room due to staff shortages. By the time the fire was noticed, there was little the hospital fire brigade could do, it was reported at the time.

The enormous central building was riddled with structural faults, as well as being built on an unstable cliff top. It was demolished in the early 1970s after the last of its patients had been moved to a new mental hospital built at nearby Cherry Farm, a much jollier name for such an unjolly sort of place.

I didn't learn about those lost girls, the dead second cousins of mine, until I was 30 or more. I'm not even sure how they came up, probably in passing and by accidental reference, as old family secrets sometimes do. My Great-aunt Gertrude was their mother and Auntie Gert was years dead by the time I heard the story, and my grandmother, her sister, was dead, too. My mother was slow and a bit vague with any details. It seemed such a sad story.

When I was young and we were living in Dunedin, we'd sometimes visit my great-aunt in her spooky old house hidden sunless behind hedges up on a hill in one of the city's strange old suburbs. She was a little, busy Scottish woman in an apron, and was always overjoyed to see us, fussing over my younger brother and me, offering us homemade cordial and biscuits, all the time telling us not to be frightened of Georgie, our second cousin, who generally wouldn't emerge from the shadows of the house until we'd been there long enough for us to have relaxed a little.

Then he'd suddenly be there, usually waving something at us, and grunting excitedly and frightening the wits out of us, especially my little brother. I always managed to keep myself a little braced for Georgie, but he'd still make me jump. He was 12 or more years older than me, and big in his misshapen jumper and old-man trousers and slippers. There was something wrong with his mouth, twisted with thick scars running upward from his top lip to his nose.

He didn't have any words at all, and he'd grunt and snort at us, waving whatever he was holding for our attention. Often it was a frayed clutch of his mother's old *Woman's Weekly* magazines tied together with a string at the corner.

Georgie would point out pictures in them, all excited to have company, making his frightening noises, Aunt Gert hushing him to calm down. He had no top in his mouth, my mother had told me, and as he stood over me trying to say something, I'd try not to look up into it for fear I might see his brain squirming in there.

There'd be tea and scones, and Aunt Gert would usually try to give my mother money. I recall her pulling a pot out of a cupboard, popping off its lid and revealing a nest of pound notes she said she'd taken from my Uncle George's pockets. He wouldn't miss them, she said. When my mother wouldn't take the money, my aunt would try to slip some into my pocket as we were leaving.

I hardly ever saw her husband, my Uncle George. He was a Communist, my grandfather said, making that sound nearly as bad as being a Catholic. Once, my grandparents came home a day early from their Christmas holidays to find Uncle George filling a sack full of fruit and vegetables from their garden. That's how Communists behaved, apparently.

No one ever said anything about there being other children besides Georgie, who I don't think I ever saw again much after we moved south from Dunedin to Invercargill when I was eight. Then, 20 or more years later, my mother let the family secret slip, and of course I grabbed at it and wanted more, but she couldn't tell me much, though she told me a little.

My great-aunt had had three girls before she had Georgie, and there was something wrong with every one of them. The first died soon after being born in the 1920s. The other two, born only a few years apart, lived, though they were simple-minded in some unspecified way. When they reached their teens their father feared some passing stranger would take advantage of them and get them pregnant, so he had them put away in Seacliff, just down the coast from their home on the chicken farm in Hampden.

Then a few years later Aunt Gert gave birth to Georgie, and, though he was maybe the most handicapped of them all, his father insisted he stay home in the care of his poor mother.

It was because he was a boy and his father couldn't have a boy put away, my mother said. He didn't care about the girls. He was a hard-hearted man, she said. And a Communist, of course.

I had only the vaguest memories of him. I saw him just a few times. He was tall and lean and wearing a hat maybe. But all the men wore hats then, except my father, who hated hats. My uncle didn't seem to be one of those men who liked kids. He made me a little nervous, I recall. Maybe it was just that he didn't say much. Maybe it was the Communism.

He wouldn't let Georgie be schooled or seen to by outsiders in any way, though he and my aunt had supposedly been told that there was a good chance some of his awful handicaps might have been made at least a bit better by surgery. My uncle got money from the Government for keeping the boy at home. At least that's what I was told.

After my aunt died, aged 81 in the winter of 1984, my uncle straight away put his beloved boy into the care of the psychiatric health system, or what remained of it by then. The old Seacliff asylum had long since been closed, replaced by Cherry Farm, named not because the fruit grew there, but after a local mariner, a Captain Cherry.

Georgie would have been transferred there. But then Cherry Farm closed, too, in 1992, at which point he was moved into Dunedin and a mental-hospital unit there. He died in 1999, his occupation listed on his death certificate as 'invalid'.

In the absence of any interest in his remains, after cremation his ashes were returned to the funeral director, who was based in Balclutha, of all places. Georgie's ashes could be sitting on a shelf there to this day, waiting to be claimed.

I found all this out years after the events. An online search of Dunedin's cemeteries' records revealed my aunt was buried in a plot at Andersons Bay Cemetery with two of her daughters: Catherine, who died in 1936, and Veronica, who was 37 when she died in 1966. There's no mention of the other, older girl.

The last time I visited Seacliff, what was left of the old asylum had been turned into a lodge for backpackers. Those backpackers would have had to be seriously lost to be on this road. But the lodge is gone, and now the gate is festooned with signs saying *Keep Out, Private Homes*.

Adjoining the site, just down the hill, is a reserve named for the asylum's most famous superintendent, Truby King, and, if you wander in far enough, past the specimen trees King planted all those years ago, you'll find shattered remnants of parts of the walls of the great mad castle that was the Seacliff Lunatic Asylum and, across a fence and up the rise, some of the outbuildings, still upright.

On the corner of the road, down the hill below, there's an ancient rusted Humber car sitting parked up with a faded *For Sale* sign in its milky window. In our car, Babybird are singing 'Drug Time' again. It seems to be our theme song and, increasingly, it makes sense.

We're rolling down into Karitane, a scattered village, much of it hidden in winding one-way lanes behind vast, tightly trimmed macrocarpa hedges, some with gateway arches cut through them to the houses behind; one we spot styled as a garage, car parked inside. Karitane might be the prettiest seaside settlement in Otago, and that's saying something. But it's a hard place to penetrate, to get a total sense of, twisting in on itself, hiding behind those hedges, really only opening out for the wide, lovely estuary it borders.

Truby King lived here with Mrs King and the kids when he was the superintendent of the Seacliff Mental Asylum,

up the road behind us. King was a remarkable man and a bit of a master of multi-tasking. As well as superintending those 500 certified lunatics, he was busy making plans for improving the health and life expectancy of the nation's babies by setting up the Plunket Society.

He was also very enthusiastic about gardening. It's his plantings that have long kept the Karitane peninsula well connected to the mainland. He'd only just built his two-storey, twin-gabled family house, Kingscliff, on the peninsula around the turn of the twentieth century when he became worried that the river would push through the narrow connecting strip of land and turn his peninsula inconveniently into an island.

He bullied the locals into building sea walls, widening the land and planting hardy gum trees on the isthmus, to the extent that, today, you'd never know that the peninsula was once so fragile. Kingscliff still stands there, white with a flagpole, occupied now by another family.

King, who was later knighted, ran the asylum at Seacliff for 30 years from 1888, and tried, to some extent, to bring enlightenment to the dark place which had previously been run pretty much as a prison for the insane, which the young nation seemed to breed in some numbers. The asylum's warders, posing for the camera in old photographs, look positively thuggish, all hard-eyed, moustachioed and bursting with beef under their tunics.

Truby King wasn't entirely an angel either. Some of his methods make alarming reading. Just a couple of years after he'd taken over at Seacliff, according to historian James Belich in his book *Paradise Reforged*, King dealt with an

'inveterate masturbator' who must have been bothering them at the asylum by having her ovaries and clitoris removed by one of his surgeons. 'Dr King's idea being as far as possible to obliterate the whole of the genital tract,' said a report.

Male masturbators got off much easier at the time, being more commonly treated with electro-shock therapy to the testicles. As a result, there were probably very few wankers in New Zealand in the 1890s, though I'm not sure anyone was keeping a record of that sort of thing at the time.

Years back, on one of my earlier visits to the site of the old asylum when there were no gates and 'keep out' signs, I was poking around in the old outbuildings and stumbled on a room piled with a dusty jumble of what looked like old shock-treatment gear, dials and cables and beds with straps attached.

Apart from King, and Janet Frame of course, another resident who became famous was Lionel Terry, a homicidal white supremacist who was committed to Seacliff in the early 1900s, when Truby King was long settled in, running the place. Terry, an upper-class Englishman, had travelled across New Zealand lecturing on the evils of the Chinese race, whom he had taken a fierce umbrage against for some reason.

The hard-working Chinese had come to New Zealand in considerable numbers to work the goldfields, and many stayed on. Terry wrote a book of poetry, *The Shadow*, railing against them, but, when no one took much notice of his racist ravings, he travelled to Wellington where he quite deliberately shot dead a 68-year-old Chinese man, Joe Kum Yung, on a city street to make his point. Out of some self-delusion of mercy, Terry deliberately chose an older, infirm victim.

When he wasn't immediately tracked down and arrested after the killing, he walked into the Lambton Quay Police Station, put his revolver and a copy of *The Shadow* on the counter and confessed. 'I have come to tell you I am the man who shot the Chinaman in the Chinese quarters of the city last evening,' he said. 'I take an interest in alien immigration and I took this means of bringing it under public notice.'

On his way to the police station, Terry had asked a Lambton Quay bookseller how *The Shadow* was going, and, when told sales were slow, he said, 'It will sell better tomorrow', which of course it did.

He was sentenced to death after a sensational trial that excited a national wave of anti-Chinese feeling. The sentence was commuted to a life sentence after Terry was later judged to be insane, but when he set fire to his prison cell and caused trouble in the Christchurch asylum to which he had then been transferred, he was packed off to Seacliff where he continued to be a handful, escaping several times into the arms of his many supporters, who had raised a petition with 50,000 signatures calling for his release.

Truby King sorted the situation by offering Terry some limited freedom in return for him agreeing to stop escaping, which he did. The infamous madman was given a suite of rooms at Seacliff to use as bedroom, library and studio.

When he refused to eat foreign foods, he was also given a garden so he could grow his own. He wrote his poetry, painted, made wine and walked the hills with his pet goats and sheep, which he'd trained to come at his call.

In a final adventure, before eventually dying in 1952 aged 79, Terry reinvented himself as a born-again Jesus, growing his hair and beard long and getting about in robes or an ice-cream-coloured suit he favoured for his outings, though his freedom was limited again in 1940 when he attacked one of the asylum's doctors who made the mistake of approaching him with a large syringe.

A copy of *The Shadow* is hard to find these days, but some of Terry's poems and paintings can be found at the little museum up the road from Seacliff in Waikouaiti. The arc of his madness can be traced through his poems — his early efforts sweet and sylvan, the later ones fizzing with mad rage.

*O sweet is the music that ripples and trills*
*From the song of the linnet in May,*
*And sweet is the scent of the dew dappled rose*
*At the dawn of a mid-summer's day.*

And, just a few years later:

*I am a man, I hold the right*
*To follow reason's light*
*And I will fight with all my might*
*To keep my nation WHITE.*

The capital letters are Terry's. It was with the publication of *The Shadow* that the craziness really seemed to kick in, though it's unclear what set off his hatred of other races.

*See, advancing grim, relentless as a scourge sent*
*forth from hell*
*Comes the blighting curse of Mammon, in the*
*white man's land to dwell*
*Mongol, Ethiop, nameless horror, human brute*
*from many a clime*
*Swathed in rags in noisome odours, gaunt and*
*fleshless, dwarfed of limb*
*Visaged like the grisly jackal seeking dead midst*
*shadows dim*
*See the hordes of drug besotten, sin begotten fiends*
*of filth*
*Swarming o'er thy nation's bulwarks, pillaging thy*
*nation's wealth.*

Awfulness aside, the 'drug besotten, sin begotten' line is rather good. But, finding that merely writing about it wasn't sufficient to expiate his racist urges, Terry set out in 1905 to commit his murder. And he went about it in a strange and relentless way, embarking on an epic walk that took him almost the length of the North Island, starting in Mangonui and getting him, footsore, to the capital city 40 days later.

A policeman in Lower Hutt noted his arrival in Wellington, telling the court during the murder trial that 'He looked a perfect picture, as fine a man as ever I saw, bolt upright and with as free an action as you'd ever see in a trained athlete.'

Behind bars, Terry's poems kept coming, undiminished and relentless in their belief.

*For four long years he wrote and spoke*
*But no-one cared a button*
*The public mind could not be raised*
*Above the price of mutton*
*So taking his revolver*
*To Wellington's foul slum*
*He sent a crippled Chinaman*
*Let's hope, to Kingdom come!*

Though, as the years went by, some humour crept into his verse.

*But Lionel Terry did not like*
*The mental institution*
*He got away and found the change*
*Improved his constitution.*

As Gordie drives us out beyond Karitane back towards Highway 1, we spot black swans in a field, which gets us talking of the time Gordie's country cousin Fred turned up at the flat with a swan he'd shot and thought I might like to cook us all for dinner while they knocked off a few beers.

I was the designated house cook, after all. The attractive trade-off for being king of the kitchen was that I did no dishwashing and no housekeeping. I don't think I even had to make my bed.

I'd thought it was a pretty sweet deal until that swan turned up. After that experience, my only advice about eating swan is: don't. Goose is gamey, swan is way beyond. But we were usually hungry and short of cash back then, so that swan was dinner — and several more dinners beyond, the last few curried in a desperate bid to quell the powerful swan taste. Then we threw the leftovers out. There's an awful lot to a swan.

Now we're off that loony-bin loop road and back on Highway 1, sailing north through undulating close-shaved fields. Here comes Waikouaiti, where, apart from the madman Lionel Terry's poems and paintings, there's a lovely racetrack. The trainers exercise their horses on the beach, which is just down a side road from the little town, which actually has quite a large claim to fame being the so-called birthplace of Otago.

This is where the first white settlers came ashore, and it was the main port for the area until they cut a decent road south to Dunedin and it started getting all the attention. That's when Waikouaiti upped and moved away from the sea to resettle itself around the main road, and it grew from there into what it is today, which isn't a great deal: population 800 or so, plus horses.

Though I'm not here to look at the horses. I'm a little nervous around horses, perhaps as a result of growing up in a horsey part of Invercargill. Where we lived was just around the corner from Racecourse Road, which, unsurprisingly, was home to the Invercargill Racecourse.

And all around us, in the new suburb's streets, were racehorse stables. There was a Jockey's Hotel out on the main road, and a blacksmith, just down from the dairy, though there's no evidence now that they ever existed. I was friendly with the sons of a horse trainer who lived right across the road from us. The boys' mum was gone, I'm not sure where, and their dad was a bit of a drinker, so it was fish and chips for dinner most nights over there, if they were lucky.

Their dad had parties for the racing crowd, and they were a fast crowd, as the straight folk used to say in those days. In our suburb, Hawthorndale, most folk were pretty straight. But that fast racing crowd was interesting to some of us, the dodgy-looking guys with their shiny suits and their big American cars, and women with big eyelashes and tight dresses.

They'd play Elvis Presley records on the radiogram, dance and grope each other and get really drunk. We curious kids would be keeping a close eye on things from the shadows. Later, my pals would sometimes pick their face-down fathers' pockets and wave their loot at me. Poor buggers, I used to think, even then.

Their grandfather, who lived in the house behind theirs with their rickety old grandmother, was a horse trainer, too, but not a drunk one. He was a scary old bugger who once chased us with his horsewhip, for something he thought we'd done. I still remember running hell for leather across a field of high grass with that whip cracking behind us. They were hard people and hard on their high-spirited racehorses, and, it seemed to me, the horses were nasty right back, given the chance.

We neighbourhood kids would be roped in occasionally to help with the horses, usually when they were trying to round up the young stallions they'd graze in nearby fields when it was gelding time. I remember a vet laughing as he threw a screaming horse's bloody balls at us.

We'd hang out, too, down at the racecourse on race days, collecting empty beer bottles to sell to the bottle man, and pinching full ones if we got the chance, to sell to the old guy on the gate who didn't care where his next drink came from.

Every time I see a horse up close now I feel nervous, but it's not the horse's fault, and they do look handsome in a field at a distance.

And now we're in the slightly bigger town of Palmerston, though we shoot straight on through for an off-piste visit to Shag Point, a strange spot where they used to mine coal in shafts that stretched out below the floor of the sea. There's little sign of the mining history now. Tourists visit to see the seals, which loll about like big over-stuffed sleeping bags on the rocks below. There are dozens of them and they don't care about us.

I don't care all that much about them. Seals are a dime a dozen on this coast, and I'm more interested in the old mines anyway. Those are the miners' old shacks still sitting there, lining the skinny road down the coast out to the point, but now they're holiday cribs for the well-to-do from Dunedin.

There seems no interest in raising any monument to the old coal industry that once must have dirtied up the place. There's not even a sign with some old photos and historical notes at the end of the road where the mines were. Just seals, but underfoot there are fragments of coal glittering darkly on the walking path.

A rugged local, who, by the look of that rod on his shoulder, is off to throw out a fishing line from the cliffs, confirms the coalmine story in an abrupt sort of a way. 'You're standing on them,' he says when we ask. And the shafts did run out under the seabed, but they weren't well built, and after the mining stopped they collapsed and the sea flooded into them. There's moki and cod out there to catch, says the bloke. An icy wind whips at us as he clomps off in his loose gummies.

Back in the car I tell Gordie, 'Time for a mutton pie in Palmerston.' I can't go through Palmerston without stopping for a mutton pie, even though I know heartburn lurks 20 minutes down the road afterwards. I have to have a mutton pie for my father. He loves them. Or he used to.

Dad used to get the people in Palmerston to send him a box of their pies every now and then. He'd keep a stock of them in the freezer and re-order when they ran low. He'd buy their 'seconds', the ones that were misshapen or had a little break in the pastry. They gave him a good price for those.

Also known as a Scotch pie, the mutton pie is a remarkable greasy and peppery affair wrapped in a stiff short-crust pastry and best eaten with a liberal splash of Worcestershire sauce. You won't find them much in New Zealand outside Otago and Southland, where they're still loved by anyone with a trace of Scottish blood in them. Gordie's Irishness is holding him back from such feelings.

But I drag him into McGregor's Pies in the main street of Palmerston, where their specialty is the mutton pie and their motto is *Baking Kiwi Pies at Sparrow Fart Since Adam was a Cowboy*. We buy one each, and I insist Gordie takes a nice photo of his one, sitting atop one of the tables out in front of McGregor's, before he takes a bite.

He sets it up, takes a nice snap, picks up the pie, has a bite, scowls and bungs it in the bin, right in front of the shop. 'You've just committed a major cultural sin,' I tell him, but he doesn't care. I hope the ladies in the pie shop didn't spot that. Gordie's getting back in the car. We're off.

Palmerston is where we turn from Highway 1 onto Highway 85, which will take us up to the Maniototo region. There's a sign for *Horse Poo $1 a Bag* on the roadside just

outside town. You don't get those sorts of offers back in the big city.

Beyond a place called Dunback, we take another side road, to Macraes Flat, where there's a whacking great open-cast goldmine I thought we could have a look at, and a nice old pub, though we won't be stopping for a beer. There will be no beer 'til Naseby.

The landscape's changing, the ground looking drier and rockier the more the road rises into the enormous sky that enfolds this high desert land. Wilding pines are making their fatal mark in little groves out there, unwanted, maybe unstoppable. And there, visible ahead of us like some sort of crazy movie set, are the great scars of the Macraes mine, its tailing arranged in great walls.

The mine operation has been scaled back a lot since the gold price fell. We stop for a look at the great pit the goldminers have dug. It's like an uglier and less grand Grand Canyon. If there were trucks at work, they'd look like toys down in the distant bottom of it.

Back on the road, we come upon the tiny town of Macraes Flat. The only retail, the only anything much at all, is the nineteenth-century stone pub, Stanley's Hotel, and, out in some fields nearby, an odd and lonely art project I wouldn't have known to go looking for if Gordie hadn't known, probably from some colour story he organised for the news on TV3.

The art installation consists of billboard-sized artworks of varied style and intent, some of the intent obscure. One piece, way across the other side of the dry field, simply says *Men*, but darkly somehow.

It's weird around here, and it gets even weirder a few kilometres west of Macraes Flat, where we drive upon an unsettling sight on that high, lonely road, where we see no other cars, or indeed signs of life, save the recently-dead.

Without notice or warning, the barbed-wire fence that follows our side of the road becomes festooned with dead pigs, wild hairy ones, their skins and heads, hung noses-to-tails along the top wire. I know there's a bra fence in another part of Otago and there are fences of sneakers, but a pig fence is a new experience, even for Gordie, who's much more rural than I am.

The pig fence goes on and on. It's so impressive that we turn around to drive back slowly and measure it, figuring it by the distance between the fence posts multiplied by the number of posts. There's half a kilometre of dead pigs here. At the eastern end, they're older, bleached and desiccated

by the sun and the dry winds, skulls showing through their hairy hides here and there, while at the western end, they're relatively fresh. Gordie insists we do a count and, figuring for the average number of dead pigs between those evenly spaced posts, there are around 350 deceased porkers hanging out west of Macraes Flat.

Slightly unsettled, we drive on, the strange landscape taking us down to meet the Middlemarch road. Walls of layered rocks rise from the land like castle ruins. The heartburn from the mutton pie has kicked in and we're not even in Ranfurly yet.

This is where the railway came through in the old days. These days, the rails have been ripped up and it's a famous rail trail, popular with the older set, who cycle where the trains used to run, and stay nights and eat meals and drink and buy small souvenirs and bring life back to tiny old gold towns like Oturehua and Clyde. 'I biked this,' says Gordie.

We cross the Taieri River and turn right onto Highway 87 and a town called Hyde, which is a pub, a scattering of houses and a trucking company, its yard full of dusty blue trailers and trucks. Beyond, dull green-brown hills across Capburn Stream, the rail trail out to our right, following us.

A sign announces we are now officially in the vast and varied desert that is Central Otago. But specifically, we're in the part called the Maniototo, a haunting place where the land arcs up towards the sky and the hills always seem to lurk in a far-off haze. It hypnotises some people, like Janet Frame and several painters, especially Grahame Sydney, who lives up the road ahead, in a nice house he had built a little way outside St Bathans.

We're passing through tiny Kokonga, where there's a backpackers for the two-wheel tourists and that's about it. Beyond, the road drops to the flats. Gordie used to come here when he was living in Christchurch, for the duck shooting, he says. Gordie's always been an enthusiastic duck shooter, I recall. I've only ever been duck shooting once, and it was with Gordie as it happens.

It was a Sunday morning in 1970, and well before the worshippers started arriving at the big old church across the road from our flat. We headed out in the dark hours before dawn, having stayed up all night, post-party.

There were four or five of us in our shooting party, including one of our fellow reporters, an Englishman as tall and thin as John Cleese and, as it turned out, somewhat more dangerous.

Despite his physique, or perhaps because of it, he drove one of those tiny cars of the time, a Fiat Bambina. It had a sunroof and sometimes, in search of a laugh, he'd pop his head out of it as he drove away. It was his first time duck shooting, too, and he seemed keen to start blasting. Despite Gordie's best efforts, we came home duckless.

We got bored out there sitting by a pond in the sticks trying to stay warm. We go so bored that we shot at an innocent tree until it fell down, and John Cleese blew apart a poor goose that wandered out of some farmer's field and into his line of sight. He may have shot one or two of its goosey friends, too. The discretion of memory has blanked the details. All I remember is a lot of feathers and blood and the shotgun roaring. It was a bad scene, and we didn't even take home for dinner what was left of the poor geese.

When Highway 87 abruptly ends a little way up the road, we turn left near Kyeburn, where there were old gold diggings, picking up Highway 85, the main road from Palmerston, again. Now we're not that far from Naseby, where we have a date booked for a few rounds of that odd sport curling, another thing Gordie's keen on, though his passion for curling is all my doing apparently. Up to this point in my life, I've managed to avoid playing the strange game, but it's time to loosen up.

We turn off the main drag onto Channel Road, a dusty choice and a back route to Naseby. We take the gravel road because I want to get some heroic photos of the filthy Falcon, booting off up a rise towards those far hills. It's a perfect setting, broom in yellow flower lining the road. We turn up a side road off the back road, disturbing some rabbits, who probably weren't expecting traffic. The hills around here are alive with rabbits.

Our destination pops up quite suddenly. *Welcome to Naseby, 2000 ft above Worry Level* says the sign outside town. Why have I taken so long to get back here? I ask myself.

Naseby's a gem of a place, tucked away at the end of a choice of back roads to the north of the much-less-charming Ranfurly, on the main road with all its art deco architecture. Ranfurly will never be as groovy as it wants to be. All the art deco buildings wouldn't even be there if it wasn't for an arsonist burning down chunks of the town in the 1920s and it being rebuilt in the style of the time.

Naseby, on the other hand, still feels like the older Central Otago, the gold-town one, with the added dimension of shade from the fierce summer sun, thanks to the mighty fir trees planted long ago by the town's far-sighted settlers, who gathered hastily here for the gold discovered in a gully about a kilometre from where the town is now.

At its gold-fevered peak, there were 5000 people in Naseby, where now there are maybe, just maybe, a couple of hundred. The place is still rich with original buildings, though, and, with barely a rich man's mansion in sight, Naseby remains more of the past than the present. With no through traffic, on a still day the place seems as if it's asleep.

Gordie made the bookings and got the last room going. We're sharing a one-bedroom unit at the Naseby Lodge, where Gordon has stayed in recent years when he's been in town for the curling.

I'll be sleeping on the sofa in the sitting room, and that's just fine. The lodge is fully booked and there are some flash cars parked around the place. 'That one,' Gordie reckons, 'is worth over $200,000.'

'I'd rather have the Falcon,' I tell him.

We dump our bags, splash our faces and wander downtown for a beer, past a café in what might have been the general store once. Gordon is drawn to a shambolic freelance museum in an old falling-down house across the wide road. He's been here before.

'Brace yourself,' he tells me, walking in.

Around the back there are a few old English cars in various states of home restoration, and here comes the intense old coot who curates and lives in the place. He gestures us inside his house-museum, and things turn a bit more Gothic. There's something smelly bubbling in a dirty old pot on the potbelly. It might have been bubbling for days. There's stuff everywhere, vast numbers of toys and model cars. It's a hoarding situation. We don't linger.

There are two pubs in Naseby to choose from: the Royal at the far end of one of the town's two main drags, and, around the corner, the Ancient Briton. Gordie says he has to steer clear of the Ancient Briton.

'There was a curling incident,' he says mysteriously.

'A what?'

Gordie sighs.

It seems that a few years back, one of the teams found itself a man down for the final of some important curling cup or other, and Gordie, who was staying in the pub at the time, volunteered to step up and play. He was only trying to help.

'But I played like shit,' he says, 'and because of me we lost the game.' As a result, the favourites, the Ancient Briton team, saw the cup slip from their hands. They stopped liking him so much after that, he reckons. There was some sort of unspoken mean-spiritedness that made him feel unwelcome. So we go to the Royal for our drink.

But there's nothing regal about the Royal, where the barman looks like an old brawler, his broken nose in crooked profile against the sun slanting through the low window of this low place. This pub is old, but not as old as the Ancient Briton, which, despite Gordie's misgivings, seems to be a more salubrious joint and no one mentions the curling incident when we walk in.

The Ancient Briton dates from 1863 when the place would have been full of whisky-maddened miners. The oldest bit of the Ancient Briton was built from mud bricks. There's a strange piece of old furniture, a round billiard table, in the corner of the bar, and the walls are covered with photos of great curling contests down the many years. There's a cabinet with curling cups, but Gordie steers clear of that.

Anyway, we have time for only one beer before we have to head off for the walk to Naseby's crowning glory, its all-weather, covered curling stadium, which sits by the road in the forest just out of town.

Naseby's surrounded by forest — planted originally for fuel, shelter, shade and building materials. The forest, and especially the gigantic firs by the town's park, give the perfectly-flat Naseby a slightly *Twin Peaks* vibe.

Gordie breaks the spell. He's been at his phone again, and announces he now has 253 Twitter followers.

'It's rising all the time,' he says.

'It's out of control,' I tell him. 'I don't know how you sleep.'

It's quite a long walk out of town between all the towering trees before we come upon the imposing but utilitarian-styled Naseby curling centre with its capacious car park. I've smoked a whole joint without meaning to. I felt it was necessary to help me into a curling mood.

Gordie's booked us in for an hour or two, which seems both vague and generous, though he's already saying we can leave when we want should we suddenly, for instance, need another beer. Surprisingly, there's no bar at the curling stadium. I'd been under the impression that curling was best done with a bottle of whisky in the other hand. I'm certain that's what the free-range curlers still do when they play on the frozen ponds and lakes in these parts in winter. But not at the stadium apparently.

And what a strange game curling is, dating back in Central Otago to the late 1870s, but dating back much further in the cold northern realm the game came from, which is Scotland, naturally. The oldest curling club in the world is the Royal Caledonian Curling Club, which formed in 1795. The game also has a cult following in the colder parts of America, Canada and Sweden.

Curling is basically lawn bowls on ice, involving the manoeuvring of small boulders with handles on them. It's quite mad and not remotely glamorous. For a start, they make us wear ugly rubber overshoes so we won't skate around on the ice while we're trying to slide those boulders, which, by the way, are 20 kilos and so heavy you don't actually lift them for fear you'll snap your spine.

After some lessons for me from one of the staff, we play four games. It's quite hard work and involves the activation of several muscle groups I didn't know I had. After the third game, Gordie mutters, 'They also call it the roaring game,' though I hear 'roaring' as 'boring'. It's called roaring for the noise the boulders make as they skate across the ice.

I believe we were running 2–2 when we walked out, but curling was indeed so boring that I barely remembered the score moments later.

We wander back into town, both smoking. Suddenly aware it's our last night away together, I start babbling about what a great trip it's been and all, and what good company he's been, apart from the business with the duck confit in Dunedin. But Gordie doesn't say much, though he has a certain way of not saying much that feels like he's saying a lot. I'm just not sure what. Some beer might help.

We decide to head back down to the Ancient Briton for a drink before dinner, which we're booked to take at the Naseby Lodge, where Gordie says they do a good meal. On the way back to the pub, there's no avoiding the Naseby War Memorial, marking the First World War with a list of the local boys killed and a large souvenir, a Trophy Gun, a 77-millimetre artillery piece that could lob a 6-kilo shell 10 kilometres.

After the war, in recognition of the sacrifice of lives in little places all over New Zealand, guns like this one were despatched to various locations, like Naseby, where they keep their old gun in very nice condition, freshly painted and graffiti-free.

Back at the pub, Gordie's hearty style isn't going down entirely well with some of the locals who are lounging about outside. I might not be helping. My clothes might be a little flamboyant for these parts. Saying gidday doesn't bring any echo, and one wobbly-eyed farmer in particular looks like he might be considering some sort of violence if Gordie keeps on trying to warm them up, asking him and his surly mates about the local lambing averages. They can tell we're just big-city types, no matter how much Gordie keeps referring to his rural upbringing.

We step indoors where there's quite a crowd, including a table of bowlers dressed in their whites, drinking beer poured into small glasses from big old-fashioned quart bottles. We're the only tourists by the look of the faces, the styles and the easy camaraderie between the blokes, mostly, crowding at the bar.

The one behind the bar, Adrian, is friendly, an ex-Aucklander, he tells us, fallen from the fast life of finance into something slow and sure way down here at the other end of the country. When I ask for a gin, he offers me one he reckons I'll like. It's called Rogue. 'It's made in bloody Ponsonby,' he laughs.

A face in the crowd, a taller, older one, spots Gordie. He's Dave Crutchley, the low-key local lord of the manor, who knows Gordie from previous visits and seems a bit put out that we didn't let him know we were coming to town. Dave owns the district's big station, but seems to mingle easily with the crowd of country characters in the Ancient Briton.

One drink turns into several before we can extricate ourselves to leg it back to the lodge for dinner. The food's good there, but the company's odd. There's a big table near ours making noises like an end-of-year work party. Gordie casts an eye at them.

'See that one?' he asks me, nodding at a bloke in glasses holding his workmates' attention with a story. 'I recognise him, though he doesn't know me,' says Gordie. 'I'm sure his name's Fred. I'm going for a pee.'

Gordon wanders off in a deliberate arc towards the table, walking that country cop walk of his. Just as he passes them, he turns his head. 'Gidday, Fred,' he says, not breaking his stride. Fred looks up at him with an unsure smile and loses track of his story.

We don't bother with dessert and duck back down to the Ancient Briton, where the atmosphere has moved up several notches to rowdy. Get a few drinks in them and these quiet rural types turn loud and even passionate, though they seem a different tribe from ours. In the end, the common ground runs out and so do we.

Outside, on the wander back to bed, the ground seems less certain and we have to take care walking, though traffic doesn't appear to exist in Naseby. I wish it was bigger so there was further to walk and more time left before tomorrow. But we're drunk and we've run out of entertainment options in Naseby, and next thing we know we're back at the lodge.

'I'm going to sleep now,' shouts Gordie, retreating to the bedroom, leaving me to unwrap my sofa bed and, Jesus, it's a thin thing. Never mind, I'm well anaesthetised.

# SUNDAY

We awake to a glorious big blue day outside our designer tin hut at the Naseby Lodge, and to the sound of Gordie trumpeting and bellowing at it from his room. My sofa was a bit stiff, and all I can manage is a low groan before grabbing the bathroom before McBride can get to it with his enthusiastic bowels.

We want to get the most out of the last day, and we've booked a breakfast down the road at the Black Forest Café, where the owner opens early just for us and serves us coffee, bacon and eggs along with an impromptu investment opportunity. She reckons we, or someone rich we know, should buy the old hall that looms next door to her café and set it up to house the Eden Hore Fashion Collection.

Eden Hore is from the same farming family as the great New Zealand country and western singer John Hore, who had such unforgettable hits as 'My Voice Keeps Changing On Me' and had to change his last name to Grennell to release his records in America.

But, unlike Cousin John with his songs, Eden instead had a powerful attraction to ladies' fashion garments, an attraction so powerful that he ended up buying and collecting several hundred of them, along with accessories, including undies, I believe.

Anyway, the frock-mad farmer then set up a museum, which became slightly famous nationally, though not all that famous, and I don't think it made Eden rich, though that may not have been his aim.

Anyway, Eden died in 1997 and left his collection to his nephew, who in the end couldn't cope with all his uncle's dresses and sold the whole lot to the Central Otago District Council in 2013 for a handy $40,000.

The collection could well be homeless now, in the hands of the district councillors who may not know what to do with it. The woman at the café might be onto something. Naseby could just be the obvious home for Eden's frocks. They might help put Naseby even more on the map, which it isn't particularly at the moment, though it may be better off that way. The curling is probably quite enough excitement.

We head out and back onto Highway 85, cutting west again under that big sky, flat brown fields either side stretching out to the walls of mountains. The Maniototo is a haunting place and possibly haunted, too. The name is derived from Mania-o-toto, meaning 'plain of blood', because there was a bit of it spilt around here when Ngai Tahu invaded, way back before the gold and all that rushing.

Ahead of us are Wedderburn, Idaburn and, to the south down a side road, Gimmerburn, 'gimmer' being Scottish for sheep, so I suppose there must have been a dead sheep found in the local creek around place-naming time. The sun's up on the hills, the tops still licked with snow. It can snow late in the year up here.

A few years back, the wife-to-be and I were staying not far from here, at the pub at St Bathans, in the room at the front, which is supposed to be haunted. It was just a week or so before Christmas, and we woke up to the sound of drunks shouting and dancing about in the street outside our window after midnight, their voices strangely muffled. We parted the curtains to find huge snowflakes floating down, and in the morning the place was blanketed with snow, like a postcard. But snow's out of the question today.

We've set off early so that we can drift a little on our last day. Gordie's set on taking us off a side road that runs off the St Bathans Loop Road, to a place called the Falls Dam, which he says is a sight to see and one he has obviously not forgotten.

'It looks like a great bloody big bath plug,' he says. I can't wait.

It's 9am and there's not a soul to see, not a car. The road to the Falls Dam has a *No Exit* sign with a skull-and-crossbones poison warning under it.

Despite the warning, there are rabbits bobbing about in the brown grass on the dusty roadside. Fiddler's Flat Road, which we're shooting along, isn't much wider than the car, but if there's anything Gordie likes more than a winding gravel road, it's a narrow, winding gravel road — this one winding up between brown hills.

The river below us is the Manuherikia, which runs down to meet the mighty Clutha at Alexandra after running through the camping ground there and turning south towards Roxburgh and its big old dam.

During the Depression, Fred Miller, in his pre-*Southland Times* days, went goldmining in the river there as many men did, trying to earn something to feed their families when there were no proper jobs anymore.

He lived with his wife and young son in a cave above the river at Gorge Creek, moving them into an old miner's house after finding some gold. He wrote a book about it in the 1940s, called *There Was Gold in the River*.

Fred was a lovely old guy, though I don't think Gordie and I took him very seriously when we were young reporters at the *Times* and he was in the corner at his desk, filling up his fountain pen, pondering a poem or one of his columns.

I reconnected with Fred years later, in the early 1990s when I was editing an airline travel magazine. He was an old man by then, pretty deaf and a bit decrepit, but he still had a spark about him and I thought it would be great to get him to do a story for the magazine. He seemed as keen as mustard, but the story he sent me wasn't much good, his second attempt was worse, and it all ended a bit sadly and nothing was ever printed. Fred died in 1996 aged 92, a legend in Southland and in the Corner Bar at the Kelvin, wherever it is now.

Up and up we go on the dead-end road until there it is, the Falls Dam, an odd sight indeed, a little lake with its notable and notably ugly feature, as Gordie promised, a great big concrete plughole which drains water out through an underground turbine and off down to the river way below.

Having duly seen it, and being at the end of the road, we turn back.

On Highway 85, there's only an occasional truck or car as we roll down the valley towards Becks, which isn't where the beer comes from. I'm not sure much of anything comes from Becks these days. The most interesting thing about Becks probably is the fact that it and its pub sit on a spot exactly halfway between the Equator and the South Pole on the 45th parallel.

But that's hardly worth stopping for, and on we rumble, past Drybread Road, then Lauder, with its old fawn-coloured roughcast pub and an atmosphere so unsullied by cloud and magnetic interference that it's a favoured spot for scientists to launch their balloons.

Now here comes quiet Omakau, where Gordie stayed a night when he rode that rail trail. Great bands of light splash across the foothills. There are two landscapes out there now, and a distinct edge where the green irrigated fields, fed by giant irrigators, meet the land's more natural fried brown.

We zip across the Tiger Hill Overbridge, Brassknocker Road's on our right and we're on the back road to Clyde, the Old Man Range looming ahead, the occasional modern mansion peeking through the trees.

We're in a green world now. There's a surprising field of flowers, orchards, pines and poplars, which are extremely popular in these parts. There's an old graveyard behind a low stone wall, then we're into Clyde, the new part first, built to house the workers on the awful dam that now towers over the old heart of the pretty little gold town. We're running out of road on this road trip, I keep thinking.

Old Clyde's still a cute place, but that dam up there above it, holding back its world of water, unsettles some people. There are fault lines all through the gorge behind it, holding the enormous fake lake. There's constant monitoring for land movement if that's any reassurance, but there's no assuring some people. The lake stretches 20 kilometres to Cromwell, and then on far beyond that.

Up and out of Clyde and on the road to Cromwell, the hills are shaved and shaped, pimped for progress, the original road drowned down there below us under the surface somewhere. None of it looks the same as it used to when I was a kid with my family, travelling the dusty old gorge road from Clyde through to Cromwell in a hot car.

There's an unlikely sight: rowing teams out on the water far down below us, sculling in perfect formation. I have to check, but it's alright because Gordie sees them, too. Above us, dotting those high-rise hills, we can see those seismic devices. Well, I can. Gordie's busy looking at the road ahead.

You used to be able to see the old coach road on the other side of the fearsome Clutha, but I guess it's below all that still water, too. History drowned for electricity. Up ahead, a lot of old Cromwell has been drowned, too. The truth is the town died by degrees, slowly over the years, in anticipation of the dam, the new lake and a watery fate.

'Music, please,' shouts Gordon. I put on that drug song we've grown so fond of as Cromwell comes into sight, shimmering in the midday sun on the other side of all that water. The town is an ugly, efficient new version of its old self, softening a little with the years and the trees, but still not particularly loveable to anyone who remembers how Cromwell used to be.

Gordie hangs a hard left across the causeway. The town's trademark giant fruit sculpture with its great big apricot arse is looking particularly arsey today, we think, though maybe we've just been away from home too long. Gordie spends quite a bit of time taking photos of it, then on we go. Poplars, grapevines, the Wooing Tree Winery, the Cromwell Industrial Park, Cemetery Road, the Motorsport Park Museum, all whizz by.

Cromwell was once the rugged star of Central Otago, a town that used to look like a place straight out of a western movie, perched dramatically above the wild spot where the mighty Kawerau River and the even mightier Clutha River met, ending the Kawerau's run as it blended into the bigger flow.

The town had trouble getting started in the first place. Up here in the treeless high desert in the early days, there was no timber for building, never mind keeping warm in the savage winters. So, for the goldminers who'd flocked in, home was tents and huts made of sod or stone, because there was no shortage of stone.

Getting over those daunting rivers was solved when a toll bridge was put across the Clutha upstream from the town they were calling, with the usual imagination, The Junction. Later, it was named for Oliver Cromwell, the man who cut off an English king's head.

Cromwell's first mayor was a bit of a brigand, too, as well as being, possibly, New Zealand's biggest literary liar. His name was William Jackson Barry and, if you believed what he claimed in his best-selling memoir of the time, he'd been a whaler in the South Pacific, a coach driver in

Australia, a goldminer in California, a trader in Malaya and a butcher in Ballarat, among other things, before arriving in Cromwell.

He made himself a popular local legend when he set up a shop, breaking the monopoly of the town's over-priced butcher, and was voted Cromwell's first mayor in 1866 and stayed put for three terms, beloved by the locals and feared by his councillors. (He had a habit of keeping anyone who argued with him in line with his fists.)

In the late 1870s he published *Up and Down; or 50 Years' Colonial Experiences in Australia, California, New Zealand, India, China and the South Pacific; Being the Life History of Capt. WJ Barry.* Long titles were popular at the time, but the addition of 'Captain' to his name was as much a make-up as much of the content of the book, which was followed by several other so-called memoirs that also sold well, though with diminishing returns.

Barry spent his later years on the lecture circuit, illustrating his increasingly tall tales with increasingly theatrical props, including a 20-metre whale skeleton, which he carted along with him. The audiences loved him, apparently, except in Timaru, where it is recorded that they threw rotten eggs. Oh, and in Central Otago, where they were sick of him and his stories by then. He died in poverty, in Christchurch, in his late eighties, better known as an entertainer than a politician.

By the time the gold finally ran out, Cromwell had turned into a service town for the farms and stone-fruit orchards that spread out around it, loving the sun and the soil in those river valleys.

But when the news spread that a huge dam was to be built downstream at Clyde and that old Cromwell would eventually drown, the life went out of the place. Black-humoured publicans painted lines on the walls of bars indicating where the water level would be when the new lake rose, upkeep wasn't kept up, and the pretty old town took on a shabby air.

It wasn't until the end of the 1980s that the dam was completed, and Lake Dunstan rose and stilled the tumultuous rivers and covered 1400 hectares of good land and even more of the old badland.

When I was a kid on holiday at Christmas in the hot summers around here, Cromwell seemed like a town John Wayne might ride his horse into at any moment. But not anymore, not in the tidy new town with its grid design, its sensible bridge, its big fruity monument and its handy bypass.

After Cromwell, the next and last gorge is the Kawerau. The landscape here is unadjusted by man or machine, sharp and rocky, the river hidden in the bottom of the gorge it's still cutting itself. In the gold-rush days, the Kawerau was a popular spot for banditry. Travellers were robbed and beaten and sometimes worse. Bodies were found in the river.

For a while, the notorious highwayman Philip Levy lived in a hut near the gorge road, which might have caused some people to revise their travel plans. Levy was hanged for murder a few years after moving north to the Nelson area and joining a gang of hoodlums up there.

*

Roky Erickson is singing 'Goodbye Sweet Dreams' in the car, and it seems good gorge music. There's a dead forest hanging to the cliffs high above us, pines. They must have been sprayed or suffered terminal vertigo.

Gordie, having driven so carefully for 1500 kilometres or so, is suddenly wheeling the filthy Falc along like a racing ace, whizzing through the bends, the milky teal-coloured river rippling in and out of view below.

The gorge is softening now. It's greener. We're in the Gibbston 'Valley of Wine' and it sure is, with its fields of vines. Mudbrick buildings, Coal Pit Road, the Cheesery, Gibbston Winery, Chard Farm. Then the AJ Hackett Bungy on the Shotover River. Neither of us has ever jumped and it's most unlikely now.

My Morning Jacket are singing their version of 'True Love Ways', the song the great Buddy Holly recorded and dedicated to his young wife just before he died in that famous plane crash that also claimed the Big Bopper and Ritchie Valens in 1959.

Cardrona's off up to the right. It's 11 o'clock. Check-in's at 11.30. There are cyclists with their butts up in the air on the hill, then Lake Hayes, which is more of a large pond really. There's a house called The Turret, with a turret of course, and Walnut Lane, with walnut trees I imagine, and mansions. This is the land of mansions. The Lake Hayes Estate offers a sea of rooftops to gaze over. And here's Frankton and its inevitable adventure-ending airport.

It's so strange to be back where we started six days ago, wiser perhaps, certainly dustier. It seems like we've been away a lifetime.

# AFTERWARDS

My friend Sam Hunt has had several good things to say over the years about getting older, sometimes when he was still quite young. One of my favourites is a poem called 'Hitting Forty'.

*I like being this little bit older.*
*Given me more time to see the reason*
*every body has their season,*
*the shape of the cross on their shoulder.*

*I like being this little bit sadder.*
*Always thought it would last forever*
*and mostly funny if not clever,*
*the first to fall off the ladder.*

*Older, sadder — but wiser, never,*
*not on these heron legs, no:*
*that's when I say I got to go*
*hit the road. Which goes on forever.*

Sam's going to turn 69 shortly, and then, I suppose, 70 an alarmingly short while after that. And here I am, just four years behind him and teetering on being something I never quite envisaged being: a pensioner. While my other old friend, Gordie, is just teetering, though not really teetering at all, strangely basked, as he is, in the light of knowing just how nigh his end is and having the time of his life with what it seems he has left.

Which makes me feel like the rest of us are just fiddling about, never getting to that bloody bucket list everyone talks about, but no one ever actually empties. Well, Gordie's about halfway through his about now, and enjoying every moment of it.

He tells me what he's been up to lately, as promised, over lunches. Last lunchtime, he had his iPad out, showing me pictures from the holiday to Turkey he and Patricia had just got back from. He returned the Turkish travel guides I'd lent him. I haven't quite got to Turkey myself. Gordie said I'd love it. Also, he said, he's given up the cigs.

It's wonderful to see my friend having a good time, but I can't shake the feeling that I'm writing my way towards a melancholy ending, though Gordie remains what I can only describe as aggressively philosophical about things.

Also, without perhaps meaning to, he has become inspiring, though that's not a word I'd use too loosely around him. And I've noticed, too, that there is a spiritual side to him, but only generally late at night, in certain conditions and in the right light.

Gordie also has his practical side. He likes to make firm decisions. He quit his job at TV3 soon after we came back from that road trip south. After learning of his health issue, he hadn't seemed sure whether he should, but then he decided he didn't want to spend whatever good time he had left at the office doing the same thing he'd been doing for years now.

'What will you do with yourself?' I asked.

'Lunch,' he said. 'A lot of lunch.'

TV3 threw a hell of a farewell party for him, and I was invited as his furthest-back friend in the business. I got a call from Patrick Gower. He told me I was to organise the music. 'Flash wants a live band,' he said, 'and he said you were the man to sort it out.'

'I'm a bit out of touch,' I told him.

'It's what Flash wants, Col,' Paddy said, without even asking if he could call me that. But it seemed as though Gordie had told everyone he thought needed to know about his health issue and, as a result, there was an unspoken bond between us all, of wanting to do right by him and for him, no matter how nutty.

So, with a little help, I found a band — a tuba, banjo, percussion and vocals ensemble, émigrés all from the Balkans or somewhere similar. They cost quite a bit and they played bent versions of old classics. They called themselves, darkly, Tequila Sunset, and they were perfect for the mood.

Later in the evening, Gordie got up and did a touch of percussion, backing vocals and dance moves with the band, and impressed those blokes from the Balkans so much that they want him to do some gigs with them, though they may say that to all the guys.

The other thing I noticed that night, before things fell a little out of focus, was how much everyone loved my grey-haired friend, from leathery old news dogs and crusty cameramen all the way through to dewy-cheeked young things, many of whom seemed to see Gordie in an almost holy light.

I wasn't surprised. I've long suspected that crazy old Christian back in Invercargill, Arnold Brooker, gave Gordie some sort of power all those years ago. It might have been in exchange for getting Arnold into *The Southland Times* office and Gordie just never mentioned it to me.

Sometimes I wish Gordie also had never mentioned his health issue to me that sunny afternoon, though of course I'm glad he did. He had to. He told me because I'm one of the people he cares about, and he knows I care about him, though we'd never say such things to each other. I'm not sure it's something men care to do, and I'm reasonably happy with that, though not totally.

Health issues are especially difficult things to talk about, and, as a result, many of us remain blissfully unaware of much of the detail of the decrepitude of most of our mates, figuring they'll tell us anything we might need to know, but probably not until the last minute, and maybe that works, but only right up to the point where it doesn't work at all anymore.

My dad didn't mention that he was going to die, well not to me, though he was 91 in the end and I knew it was only a matter of time. I could tell that he was getting a bit sick of all the hanging around and feeling like he was no use for anything anymore.

What with the tyranny of distance and all, I saw him only a few times a year, and each time there was noticeably a little bit less of him. Just a sliver gone each time, but the slivers were adding up and going past some point of no return.

Dad would get up and shuffle across the room and then not know where he was going exactly, though he'd often laugh about it. He'd drift in and out of conversations, too, so that our exchanges weren't really conversations anymore because he'd forget what he was talking about halfway through almost every sentence.

My brother told me sometime later, after the funeral, that Dad had said to him, 'I didn't know dying would be so hard.' I was glad I wasn't there to hear him say that. I'd probably have cried so much that they would have had to put me on a drip.

Like Gordie, I don't want to think about dying, and most particularly about when it's going to be my turn. I had been hoping it was going to be a bit later than sooner, though I'm not so sure anymore, and in any case the time left is whizzing by and it's been a while since my last check-up.

Check-ups aren't things I want to do too much, in the main because I remain stubbornly reluctant to do much about changing my wicked old ways of life, dropping some of the bad habits I've fallen into. As a result of this unworldly attitude, anything could happen and occasionally does.

Like, for instance, not very long ago when my old friend Sam came to Wellington to do some shows and stayed a night with us. We keep in touch and talk on the phone every few days, but we hadn't seen each other in a while. Also, it was the first time he'd seen our new house, which seemed a good reason to celebrate, which we usually do anyway when we're in the same place for any length of time. Half an hour might do it.

But maybe we overdid it a little bit this time, though it seemed like nothing compared to how we used to overdo things, and, anyway, it was apparently only me who overdid it.

Which is to say that when I came round, I was lying flat on my back on the floor, a machine was beeping somewhere nearby, there were people in uniforms in the room and Sam was kneeling next to me whispering, 'Don't go.'

'Where?' I asked, not quite knowing where I'd just been. I'd been overdoing it, apparently.

'I think I fainted,' I said to no one in particular. 'Like a Victorian lady.'

'Something like that,' said the ambulance attendant who was shaving my chest and sticking wires all over me.

'It's my friend's fault,' I said. 'He led me astray.'

'I did,' said Sam, getting back to his feet. 'It was the strong Northland bud that got him.'

'Rubbish,' I squeaked. I thought about getting up to prove that there was nothing really wrong with me, but found I didn't have the strength to raise myself from the floor and decided not to try. It was about this time I realised that, aside from fainting like a Victorian lady, I'd also peed myself, though I was wearing black jeans and hopefully no one had noticed. This wasn't a glamorous situation.

But I managed to talk the health professionals out of taking me to hospital for further tests, and Sam did 'Wave Song' and another couple of poems for them, and it all hopefully seemed like a dream to all concerned in the end.

I was keen on that interpretation. But perhaps that was a foolish thought.

The next day, when she got home from school, the 16-year-old daughter took me aside and said, without much in the way of gentle lead-up or preamble, 'Your party days are over, Daddy. You're an old man.'

And while that might seem quite rough talk and even a bit disrespectful coming from your kid, I didn't take that 'old man' bit to heart. Maddy tends to overstate things to get my attention and I'm sure she's right, though I do have memories of falling over sometimes in the good old days, before she was even thought of, and I didn't die then. Back then, I don't recall anyone ever calling the ambulance.

But of course the daughter is right and she's worried about me and my old-fashioned ideas of what constitutes a good time, and of course I want to be sensible and live forever, as promised in the unspoken pact we parents make with our children.

But, whatever we might have silently promised, we still won't get to live forever and there's no shortage of signs to remind us of our mortality, just in case we forget.

There is, for instance, a point at which, after some particular age or other, your relationship with your doctor changes, though you might not notice this at first. It's just that now, instead of actually going to see your doctor only when you're feeling bad, you start going, if you do as you're told, for regular check-ups.

This is all to be on the safe side. Well, that's what they tell you, but the truth is they've begun the search for something wrong with you. And if you're regular enough in your visits and they're rigorous enough with their checking, eventually they're bound to find something.

In Gordie's case, they found something and supposedly in time to sort it out, but in this case their treatment didn't work and things moved on from there to where they are now, which is not good.

I just heard an item on the radio saying the country's few daily regional newspapers left alive won't be having their own editors anymore. The Australian media megacorporation that owns them says it's the new way of the print media and there's no one to argue with them. This means that *The Southland Times* will no longer have an editor like the editor who hired me and Gordie that little while back.

In this bold new step towards a fucked-up future, there's going to be a regional editor at head office instead of proper editors sitting at their own desks looking out the window in those newspaper offices in those towns around the country. Things must be even sadder than they were when we visited the old office in Invercargill. And they were pretty sad then.

It seems like Gordie and I might have timed it pretty well, just right to catch the last of what we can see quite clearly now as the good old days in newspapers, and perhaps also in what followed for each of us, like television.

We both, I suppose, had a pretty good time of it and got away with quite a lot, me probably more than Gordie, but that's only because he's the newsman and I found more opportunities to drift into odd corners. I drifted into all sorts of things. I was the editor of an airline magazine for a few years, I was a restaurant critic, a fashion writer, I had a column for a while writing about bars for a big-city magazine.

For a couple of years, I was even a sharp-tongued advice columnist for *The New Zealand Herald*, pretending I was a woman called Sharon. 'Dear Sharon', the column was called. I don't recall how I pulled that one off, but I saw people reading me in cafés in Ponsonby. I made most of the letters up, real people's problems often being a bit boring. I got the push when the editor found out who was really writing the column.

I must have had a thing about advice, because a few years later I came up with the idea for a show called *Ask Your Auntie*, a down-home straight-talking Maori answer to that cynical *How's Life?* show I'd worked on. Maori TV loved it. Well, for three years they did.

I went to TVNZ with an idea for a series about books and they liked that, but they didn't like the name I'd given it, which was *The Good Word*. They said people would think it was a religious programme, and told me to come up with something better, so I said how about *The Book Show* and they loved that. They felt it caught the zeitgeist or something.

Then, when TV One dropped *The Book Show* after a couple of seasons, I took it to a channel that had just sprung up called TVNZ 7 who were keen on a book show, but not one called *The Book Show*. They said it had to be different from the old one on the other channel, so I called it *The Good Word*, and the new people in charge liked that and it ran for another five years and helped me get the Mercedes, along with quite an extensive book collection and a lot of writers' phone numbers.

I never thought any of those things would last, though. I knew from experience by then that nothing really did, but that's not such a bad thing for people who bore easily, people who wouldn't get a thing done if it weren't for the promise of money for words and the threat of a deadline. God bless the deadline and all who set their sails towards it. Without it, maybe Gordie and I would both be lost.

I interviewed quite a few people over the years, as did Gordie, but for quite a while there mine tended to be the famous rock-star types who, while you're thrilled to talk to them, have generally been asked all the questions and polished all their answers, so the resulting stories tend to be impressionistic pieces.

They'd be more about Neil Young's intense stare and crazy cackle or just how many drinks Shane MacGowan of The Pogues really could put away in a few hours between flights at an Auckland airport bar than which came first, the tune or the words.

If I was ever asked by anyone, I'd say my favourite interview was one I really only vaguely remembered. You write stories for newspapers and they're either gone the next day, never to be seen again, or turning yellow in boxes in the cellar. This particular interview was lost in the files until I found it a moment ago, an encounter with Spike Milligan, the eccentric comic genius who came to New Zealand in his later years touring a one-man show that was based very much on the mood he was in at the time.

I think he was in a good mood the day he gave me a few hours. We had lunch in a sunny apartment he was renting, and I think we drank a bit. He loved New Zealand wine and he had a large supply on hand.

It seems, reading the interview now, I thought of him as an old guy at the time and that he even agreed with me, talking as someone who was getting to the end of things, though in fact he'd go on to live for another cantankerous 20 years.

It was more than 30 years ago, that day I met Spike, who was, then, the age I am now. 'I'm a successful failure,' he told me when I asked him to sum up his life, and he meant it.

I went on to write rudely that 'At 65, Milligan is no one's idea of an elderly show biz figure. He looks fit and the disappearance of his former snowy-white beard makes him look a good ten years younger than the truth.' Cheeky young prick that I was.

The conversation turned to the stage show Spike was touring, and the fact that it was billed as his 'first farewell tour'.

'It might actually be THE farewell tour,' he told me. 'I might jack it in. I am 65 after all.'

Was he talking retirement? I asked.

'Well, professional retirement. I'll still write books and music and paint.'

Did he ever feel time was running out?

'Sometimes yeah,' he said. 'I find nostalgia becoming more a part of my life. I find myself lying in bed at night thinking about boyhood days — something I never did before.'

Did he have a favourite part of the world?

'The last place I went to I really liked was out the back in Australia. I went walkabout and discovered an old ruined farm. There were grapes growing along the ground where they'd fallen off the trellis. I found the burnt-out remains of an old buggy. There was a wonderful waterhole. I dived in.

'It was a beautiful summer's day; I was all alone. When I got to the bottom of the waterhole it was full of broken Coca-Cola bottles.

'I took my brother back there and we had a diving session to get it all out. Even there, the yahoos had made their mark.'

I asked him if, even at 65, he had any unfulfilled ambitions.

'I would still like to write and direct my own film,' he said. 'I want to do a real comedy, but the trouble is I can't argue with people. They do my shows on TV, but they don't see it the way I see it. They mean well, these directors, but they're much slower and clumsier.'

I wondered if, as he'd grown older, he'd grown more radical.

'I've always been radical I'm afraid. I'm still angry — angry about the crass stupidity of people.'

Had he ever thought about just giving up?

'I have thought, "Damn it, I won't put up with these people. I'll just speak the truth. I'll just say, 'You're bloody boring, would you mind going away?'"

'Then I thought, "No, being pleasant, being big is important. The quality of the human spirit can be enlarged by being tolerant."'

That was why he was kind even to scribblers like me, he said.

'My dad was a journalist. He always said to me, "Never turn away a journalist or a photographer. They're only trying to earn a crust."

'Most people treat journalists like wolves. But all they've come for is a bit of dirt. You know, like the dustman – "Is your bin of words ready yet, Spike?"'

# BACK SOUTH

I went back south. I had to take another sniff, I think. I
needed a few more clues and some photos of places Gordie
and I seemed to have cruised through without pausing to
take any pictures. It was odd being there without him, and
I didn't like it so much. There was a lot less laughing for a
start.

But, the truth is, it's always odd going back down there,
alone or together. It's like there's still something to settle,
something to put right, or something even to apologise for.

One of the things about the south, and Southland in
particular, is that it gets over you pretty quickly, but you
never quite get over it. And it's only once you're gone from
the place that you realise what another world it is, one you
can only visit now as a stranger, though a stranger who
knows his way around.

This time I fly into Dunedin, pick up a small and
sensible rental, a silver Corolla, drive out to Highway 1 and
turn right for Invercargill, where I've booked one night at
the Kelvin. Dunedin's airport, at Momona, is so far south

of Dunedin anyway that Invercargill seems just down the road. Well, a couple of hours down the road.

I wonder how Gordie is. He took the holiday in Turkey ahead of his next meeting with his specialist, one he might have been dreading, though he showed no signs of that. The main concern, he says, is when they'll want to start the chemotherapy. That will change things a bit in the zest-for-life department. But it will buy him time and some of that stuff the doctors refer to as 'quality of life'.

Almost all the other traffic on Highway 1 today is rolling north, and there's not much of that. It's chilly out of the car in Milton, where I stop for coffee and cheese rolls. The only other customer in the café is an old joker with a flat cap and a thousand-metre stare. He offers me his newspaper to read. Without Gordie to start it, conversation seems impossible, so I don't even try.

I pause to take a photo of that ugly bridge at Balclutha and count the arches: six. Here comes Clinton again, and its sign with the slightly dated local roading joke: *The Presidential Highway, from Clinton to Gore*. Or the other way, if you start at the other end.

Back in Invercargill on a quiet Monday and back at the Kelvin, it's Allie, the friendly barmaid from the Editor's Cut, who checks me in, gives me an upgrade, a free *Southland Times* (a thin Monday edition), and a voucher for a free drink, bless her.

Later, out on the road towards the airport, some yokel in a great big four-wheel-drive flashes his lights at me for dawdling as I drift out towards Invercargill's big ocean beach, Oreti, possibly the country's grandest beach, just in the wrong place.

It's here, fairly famously, that Burt Munro practised for setting a new world land-speed record on the motorbike he'd put together in his backyard back in town. He'd occasionally turn up at Dad's workshop down in the city, wanting a bit of welding done on various bits and pieces for his motorbike.

The blokes at the workshop thought he was a bit of an oddball, Dad said, but they helped out with the welding. Burt was so strapped for funds and spare parts for his old Indian bike that he'd have to fashion them himself, from tin cans sometimes.

Oreti Beach seems the same as it ever seemed, endless, stretching off, eventually out of focus, to the east and west of the beach entrance. Locals, as ever, are parked up on the sand, sitting in their cars gazing out at all that sea, Stewart Island floats there to the east and, straight ahead, nothing much 'til Antarctica. Just the wind.

And the people who like wind, four or five surfers, riding the long waves. We used to come out to Oreti after we'd finished work at the paper sometimes if the tide was right and there was some light from the moon, and haul out a net for flounder. Being taller, I tended to be put on the deep end of the net. It was so cold you couldn't feel yourself after a while. A great white might have taken my leg and I wouldn't have noticed.

And when I was even younger and we were still allowed to gather them, we'd come out to Oreti for the toheroa, the mythically tasty shellfish that now live safely down under the

sand, protected from any human intruders after they were, apparently, over-fished during the period I was out there with family, friends and half of Invercargill, catching them to take home and make into soup and mince into fritters.

Though catching toheroa was no easy thing. The name means 'long tongue' and toheroa do indeed have super-sized tongues, which they put to work digging down and hauling their large ivory-coloured shells deep into the sand.

They might have been a foot or so down there when you finally got hold of one. The stern and ancient rules of toheroa hunting said we were allowed to use only a wooden implement or just our hands to catch them. So it wasn't easy to get your hand on one, and once you did they'd really dig in, sometimes holding you there, bent double, hanging on, up to your elbow in soft sand with a big wave about to come right over you.

We smaller kids would try to place ourselves on the landward side of the nearest large lady so that she could break the wave and save us from being washed away. Just behind my Auntie Rita and her large bottom was always a good spot.

I'm meeting an old friend at five o'clock back at the hotel for a drink. I thought it might be interesting to talk to someone else about the old days, and this particular friend used to come to our parties back then and might remember more than me, though that may not be entirely a good thing. Time and a few drinks will tell.

I haven't really kept much in touch with him over the decades. Like Gordie, he's a farmer's son. He also, in the way of groovy Southland farmers' sons of the time, drove a Mini then, though I don't recall whether, like Gordie's, it was modified, with the fat tyres and the racing-car steering wheel and all.

He's our age and, as is often the case in our small country, he and I are bound by connections other than that long-ago one. Some of my family are friends with some of his family.

I have a little time to kill before our catch-up, so I drive out to mooch around the suburbs of my childhood and to test that theory about the persistence of memory.

There were some slightly scary streets out on the east side of town that I used to ride my bike up and down regularly when I had an after-school job delivering prescriptions for the neighbourhood chemist shop.

Those streets were full of State houses, a lot of them the utilitarian two-storey, four-unit numbers that were maybe just a bit close for the comfort of the families stuck inside them.

There was one stand-alone house in particular I recall being nervous about visiting. A blind family lived in it, or at least the mother and father were blind, but I feel like there were kids and they were blind, too. I'd always seem to turn up on my last delivery of the day when it was getting dark. The blind family wouldn't have the lights on and it was smelly in there.

They'd tell me to bring my package in down the hall to the kitchen at the back of the house and I'd have to feel my way there, like the blind family did out in the real world, I suppose. But it used to spook me, made worse by the nasty little pet dog they had that would jump up and nip at me in their dark hall.

Fifty years later, I still know how to get there without resorting to GPS, though I'm expecting to find a nice new subdivision or a big Bunnings with 3 hectares of car park. But it's just the same here now as it was then, enhanced only by the decades of decay.

I think that's the blind family's house over there. Like most of this dismal neighbourhood now, it's in a sad way. Some of the old State houses here look abandoned. At least, I hope they are. I don't like to think of anyone calling them home. Invercargill still has its dark corners, some of them looking even darker now than they were then.

Before coming south on that impulsive road trip with Gordie, I'd been back now and then, the last time on a

mission to make amends for previous crimes against the old hometown. I'd written a few snarky things about the place over the years, darkened its image, suggested maybe that the best thing to say about Invercargill was that it was a great place to leave. I might have wanted to make up for that.

I'd persuaded the *Herald* in Auckland to let me write a series for their travel section in which I'd visit and seek out the good side of some of the places New Zealanders traditionally tend to be rude about. I started with Invercargill and moved on through Ashburton, Palmerston North and Hamilton. Halfway through a second series on hard-to-love towns, I gave up.

But I thought I did alright with pushing the pleasures of Invercargill, even suggesting that, from certain angles, and in the right light of course, the long view towards the Water Tower might perhaps make a visitor think of Pisa, which could have been pushing it a bit. Still, the local tourism people told me they loved it and sent me a souvenir pen and memory stick.

Back in the Editor's Cut, the friend who never moved away turns up, and we're both so pleased to see each other that we drink a lot more beer than we'd planned to, before lurching upstairs for a drawn-out dinner with lashings more booze. 'My shout,' I tell him.

Somewhere in the middle of all the talk, my friend tells me he has a confession to make, something that's been preying on his mind, 'all these years' he says. I'm not sure I'm ready for this.

'Bloody hell,' I tell him. 'Do I need to brace myself?'

'Well, maybe a bit,' he says, looking serious. Then, after one of those long pauses that tend to occur at regular intervals in conversation with Southlanders, he gets his confession out.

He tells me to cast my mind back to those halcyon days at that flat I shared with Gordie, the one opposite the big brick church, and to one afternoon in particular. It was a sunny afternoon, he says, just like The Kinks song, and we were lying out on the roof of the garage at the front of the house, we being he and I and my girlfriend of the time. My mind's a blank.

'I don't remember.'

'You called her "the housekeeper".'

'That's appalling.'

'I think she was your girlfriend,' he says.

'Was it Jane maybe?'

'Yes, maybe. In fact, yes.'

There's another long pause before he continues with his ancient confession, which is beginning to feel like the last thing I want to hear. But there's no stopping him now.

So there we were out on the sun-kissed garage roof when I, apparently, jumped up and announced that I was hungry and going out for something to eat. At this, Jane, if indeed it was Jane, suggested I should take my friend's Mini, which was parked just outside on the road, and he gave me the keys.

But no sooner was I in the car, down the road and around the corner, he said, than she looked him in the eye and said, 'How about it?' and took him straight inside to have hasty, but obviously memorable, sex with her.

'You can't have gone far, because you came back quite quickly,' he tells me. 'We'd barely finished.'

They did it in the little room at the front of the house, the sunroom, where Gordie's cousin Fred slept when he was in town. I stop him before he goes into any more detail.

My friend looks relieved to have got all this off his chest, though I'm left not sure what to say, particularly having had no memory of any of it.

In lieu of anything better, I mutter something about forgiving him, though by the time we get to dessert I'm beginning to feel differently about this ancient treachery.

'So you had sex with her knowing she was my girlfriend?'

'Well, yes, I suppose I must have.'

'She must have had her eye on you and was just waiting for an opportunity.'

'I suppose.'

'It's probably because you had that Mini. She was never that happy on the back of my Vespa. She reckoned her legs got cold.'

'I didn't see her again.'

'You cad. It's alright. I still forgive you.'

I leave Invercargill the next morning. At least, I think I do. When it comes to Invercargill, you can never be entirely sure.